Is it ADHD?

Uncover the Link Between Temperament and ADHD to Transform Your Child's Learning, Behavior, and Relationships

Betina McConnell, Ghee McConnell

Contents

Introduction

We heard this from a couple we are friends with about their parenting journey with successfully raising a difficult kid by taking a route less traveled by other parents. Back in the day, when their kids were of school age, their daughter had no issues with memorization, concentrating, and sitting still when completing her schoolwork. Her younger brother, however, had a different experience. He could never focus, never memorize anything, hardly could stay still, and was having a hard time doing schoolwork. This was causing frustration and distress for the entire family. The parents decided to try something unusual and unorthodox that changed the direction of things. They agreed to let their son bounce on the trampoline whenever he had to memorize something. Yes! He was bouncing and studying at the same time! They introduced games and activities to help him focus and connect with the study subjects. They tailored the schoolwork and their homeschool curriculum based on their children's characteristics. The outcome was fantastic! They both became very successful. The bouncing boy was able to thrive and ended up becoming an engineer.

If you have this book, then it means that you are a parent struggling to balance it all. We wrote this book from our own experience and those we have met who have found surprisingly effective methods and strategies to parent their hyperactive and attention-deficit children. We will guide you on the nuanced journey of understanding and parenting children with ADHD characteristics and temperament differences. Discover effective strategies tailored for academic success, improved behavior, and a stronger bond with your child.

When we noticed that our daughter was constantly distracted, moving from one task to the next, we knew something was special about our child. This book is a product of our experience as parents and a few years mentoring families with unique challenges raising their kids.

Do other people and teachers at your child's school tell you your child is difficult to manage and be around? Have you found yourself tired, frustrated, and ready to give up trying to get your child to behave? Does your child struggle to stay still and focus on a task and is constantly distracted, affecting their academics and social life? But you know they have potential if only you can help them channel it correctly. If you are a parent of a child seen as problematic or diagnosed with Attention Deficit Hyperactivity Disorder (ADHD) and looking for some answers and magic solutions to help you recognize and understand your child and help them succeed in life, you are at the right place. That is exactly what you are going to find out.

ADHD and inborn temperament differences in children make them unique and special. When you read ahead, keep an open mind, willing to learn, and prepare yourself to make changes in your parenting style. There is no one-size-fits-all solution to the problems of parenting children with ADHD characteristics but rather a tailored approach. We will provide various strategies and practical, actionable advice to cater to different needs and situations. Learn, choose, and adapt what best suits you and your child. You will also read about other parents and children who walked the same path as you and came to the end, successful and happier than ever.

It is challenging to be a parent; to be a parent to a child with Attention Deficit Hyperactive Disorder (ADHD) characteristics is beyond challenging. Getting them to do the simplest of tasks is a daily struggle. It leaves you exhausted, and seeing your child struggle breaks your heart. We know the struggle; We have been there. Walk with us to embark on a journey to learn new, effective ways to become the parent your child needs and truly deserves.

Chapter 1: Decoding ADHD and Temperament

I n our family, we've observed that our sanguine temperament—characterized by enthusiasm, spontaneity, and a tendency to be easily distracted—has sometimes been misunderstood as ADHD. Our lively and outgoing nature often leads others to perceive impulsive behaviors typically associated with ADHD when, in reality, it's simply how we naturally interact with the world. This misunderstanding has highlighted the importance of distinguishing between a vibrant personality and a clinical condition. Recognizing this difference has been crucial in seeking the proper support and managing our lives effectively, ensuring we receive guidance tailored to our unique temperaments rather than a misdiagnosed disorder.

Let's explore how ADHD and temperament characteristics differ. Understanding these distinctions can help clarify how they manifest and affect behavior. By examining both, we can better understand how each impacts daily life and interactions.

ADHD: Beyond the Diagnosis

ADHD is a neurodevelopmental disorder usually diagnosed in childhood, which often lasts into adulthood and is marked by an ongoing pattern of inattention and/or hyperactivity, impulsivity that interferes with day-to-day functioning, or even development. ADHD is found to be impacting 5% of children (Drechsler et al., 2020), but many are likely going undiagnosed. Some children with undiagnosed ADHD may get diagnosed later in their adult life or may never find out the real reason for life being too difficult to navigate, even in the simplest of day-to-day tasks.

The three types of ADHD as seen in children

Predominantly Inattentive Presentation

Children with predominantly inattentive ADHD are the ones who often go undiagnosed, or their symptoms are just seen as laziness and behavioral issues. In this type of ADHD, children are not constantly moving around but lack the focus to concentrate on any given task. They may start doing something and lose interest quickly and abandon it to move on to the next thing. They have an array of hobbies and extracurricular activities they've tried, but nothing ever sticks. They are predominantly inattentive children.

Predominantly Hyperactive-Impulsive Presentation

Children with predominantly hyperactive-impulsive ADHD get noticed and diagnosed because of their evident symptoms. They cannot help but move around a lot and talk excessively. They are tagged as difficult and talkative. They act on impulse and are hyperactive.

Combined Presentation

Some children show signs of both inattentive and hyperactive-impulsive ADHD presentation. Their symptoms vary. They may be impulsive at one time and be inattentive or lose focus at other times.

ADHD affects not only the child but the entire family. ADHD reduces the quality of life for both the child and their family. Disturbances emerge in the parents and the siblings' lives, leading to disruption in the parents' marital functioning and increased bullying between siblings in families with a child with ADHD. Studies have shown that children with ADHD get less sleep and are not happy with their families and their lives in general (Peasgood et al., 2016).

The adverse effects of the neurodevelopmental disorder change from preschool to primary school and adolescence. It may persist into adulthood, causing struggles in their professional and personal lives.

ADHD often presents itself as a behavioral issue. As a result, some of the symptoms of ADHD are attributed to bad behavior and ignored. Misjudging behaviors like these as tantrums, especially in undiagnosed children, can exacerbate the symptoms. Often, the inattentive type of ADHD in children goes unnoticed and undiagnosed because, unlike the hyperactive type, it does not show any noticeable symptoms. It becomes challenging for children to focus on a task or become hyperfocused sometimes. ADHD also causes disorganization and carelessness, which will adversely affect their daily activities as well as academics.

Children with hyperactive and impulsive ADHD are not able to stay still for a significant amount of time. They can be seen fidgeting, moving around, and talking even when they are supposed to be quiet and listening, like in the classroom. They often have difficulty in adhering to rules and struggle academically, too. They lack patience and cannot help but act on whatever they feel like doing. Usually, self-control develops in children around the ages of five to six years, but in children with ADHD, it is seen to come later than usual, which may cause behavioral issues. Studies have shown mild delays in motor skills or picking up language skills in children with ADHD. They seek constant attention and act goofy for the same reason. Sometimes, children with ADHD become aggressive to other children because of their lack of self-control and hyperactive nature. It can become hard for such kids to make friends, and they risk being alienated and tagged as difficult to get along with.

Historical Context

The first clinical description of a bunch of symptoms very similar to what currently could be diagnosed as ADHD is generally attributed to George F. Still, in 1902, ADHD was not a modern disorder. Several authors have discussed Hyperactive and inattentive children in literature and even seen in some paintings during the last 200 years. Some of their early depictions have similarities to the modern descriptions of ADHD. In two of the first textbooks published by German Melchior Adam Weikard and the Scottish Sir Alexander Crichton, specifically on mental diseases, the earliest medical reports of people with abnormal hyperactivity, distraction, and inattentiveness were recorded. In the nineteenth century, eminent physicians such as Charles West, William W., Heinrich Neuman, and Thomas C. Albutt, among others, provided clinical depictions of individuals whose symptoms were similar to modern diagnoses of ADHD. Some of the children in these descriptions, however, might have suffered from other neurological and psychiatric disorders along with ADHD as a comorbidity. In 1937, the first pharmacological trials with stimulants for hyperactive children were conducted (Bradley, 1937).

Even though ADHD is a thoroughly investigated neurodevelopmental disorder, it remains a controversial diagnosis. Some argue that children who present behavioral problems at home and school get falsely diagnosed with ADHD when they are just on the extreme end of the normal spectrum. The existence of other comorbid disorders and similarities of symptoms to other factors make the diagnostic process of ADHD more difficult to achieve. Hence, it is a highly debated field of diagnosis.

Comorbidity and Complexity

For many adolescents and adults with ADHD, their functioning is complicated by one or more additional psychiatric disorders. Significant comorbidities like anxiety, depression, sleep problems, learning problems, and substance abuse are seen in people with ADHD. Studies have shown that the persistence of ADHD into adulthood may increase the risk of a Motor Vehicle Crash (MVC) when compared to childhood-limited ADHD (Roy et al., 2020). Comorbidities with ADHD impact treatment compliance and response.

The Spectrum of Temperament: A Parent's Guide

In simple words, temperament can be defined as how children respond to the world. Temperament is the early-appearing variation in emotional reactivity in children. Children's temperament traits have a strong genetic or neurobiological basis. They manifest early in life and are stable across time and situations. Temperament influences the way children interact with people and the world. It determines how they regulate their emotions and behavior and how they feel about and respond to new people and situations.

The four temperament traits

Sanguine

Traditionally, people with sanguine temperament are associated with air. People with sanguine temperament are usually lively, social, talkative, and optimistic. They are warm-hearted and make friends easily. Awakening their love for a subject and people is the best way to reach them. However, they can be flighty and change their opinions constantly. They also struggle to complete a task, are forgetful, and are chronologically late.

Choleric

Fire is the element traditionally associated with choleric people. They are impulsive, restless, selfish, and extroverted. They are ambitious and have leadership qualities. They like to get their jobs done efficiently and immediately without procrastination.

Melancholic

People with this temperament are traditionally associated with the element of earth. They are introverted, less friendly, cautious, and inclined to moodiness. They are easily affected by the tragedies of the world, making them moody and susceptible to depression. They like to do things independently to meet their standards as they are not very good with people.

Phlegmatic

Phlegmatic people are associated with water. People with this temperament are private, caring, reasonable, calm, faithful, thoughtful, and patient. They love quiet and peaceful atmospheres and are pretty content with themselves. Phlegmatic people are very consistent with their habits and can maintain good friendships. They think before they speak, so their speech appears hesitant and slow.

Temperament vs. Personality

Even though they seem similar, temperament and personality are different traits. Temperament is an innate trait that children are born with, which becomes the basis for interacting with their environments in specific ways. In contrast, personality develops over time as children grow. A study found that temperamental qualities predicted adult personalities (Caspi et al., 2003). The personality of a child is strongly influenced by innate temperament traits. Still, it is also affected by external factors like the parent's raising methods, sibling relationships, and socio-economic environment, amongst others.

Temperament has always been seen as constitutionally based on emotional and behavioral characteristics of feeling, thinking, and reacting (Allport, 1937; Rothbart & Bates, 2006). Therefore, temperament is considered biologically rooted and, hence, is determined to an extent by heredity and maturation compared to personality. Most temperamental characteristics can be seen from the infant stage itself. The baby's irritability, distress levels, and ease of soothing them are all evident temperamental traits, whereas major personality traits only emerge later in life, around the age of three. As indicated by Bornstein and Lamb (2002), their personality traits become salient over time as children experience various social situations and interact with new people, which allows their tendencies to be consolidated. With age, the temperamental characteristics in children become more differentiated and gradually integrate into their developing personality. Rutter (1987) considered this integration of temperament with personality as the projection of temperamental tendencies into the world. As per Chess and Thomas (1986), personality includes habits, values, beliefs, coping styles, and content of thought. However, temperament is majorly about the style of behavior in any situation. In the study of temperament and personality from a developmental perspective, two types of stability—mean-level stability and rank-order stability—are considered. Mean level stability is whether the average level of a trait remains the same or changes with age. Meanwhile, rank-order stability is determined by whether children maintain their relative positions on traits over time and with age. Even though various studies have been conducted, it is still unclear when and in what circumstances temporal stabilities of temperament and personality traits are maintained and when and in what situations developmental changes in these traits occur.

Impact on Parenting

Often, with the first child, parents do not notice the temperamental traits in them. However, when the second child arrives, things change. The management strategies that worked well with the first child may not work with the second child. Even the problems with feeding, sleeping, and consoling may be different with the second child than with the first child. This shows that children are born with other traits, and those differences influence their personalities. Both the parenting style and traits children are born with influence child development. Hence, our parenting style must be tailored for each child by their temperamental characteristics for a healthy childhood. Two studies influenced the theory that children are also essential contributors to their social interactions. First is the temperament research Thomas and Chess and their colleagues conducted in the New York Longitudinal Study. The other is Bell's reconceptualization of socialization between the child and the caregiver, with both trying to redirect, reduce, stimulate, or augment each other's behavior (Bell, 1968).

Rothbart said, "The infant's temperament regulates and is regulated by the actions of others from the earliest hours" (Rothbart, 1989, p. 195). Each child differs in how they respond to the parent's soothing techniques, their capacity to control their emotions, and the capacity to bring pleasure or displeasure to their caregivers.

The Inputs Between Temperaments

Brief Historical Background

The belief in the human temperament goes back a long way. Many current English words have meanings rooted in the ancient notion of humors of the body, or what we call temperaments.

The four humors are blood, choler, black bile, and phlegm. Blood was believed to govern the sanguine temperament, a word derived from the Latin word for blood. The choler or yellow bile governed the choleric temperament, the old French word for bile or anger. The black bile, which in Greek is called melancholy, governs the melancholy temperament. Finally, phlegm governs the phlegmatic temperament.

The Greek philosophers' theory was that everything in the world was made of tiny invisible atoms of pure substances, which, when mixed together, formed all the other things in the world. The earliest philosophers believed everything was ultimately from atoms of the single element of fire. Later, Empedocles' theory of four essential elements, which correspond to earth, sea, sky, and the sun, became the one that was widely accepted. When further analyzed, these four elements were found to have distinct qualities that linked them to complex substances. The air, which is moist and dry, shares the quality of moisture with water and is the opposite of the earth, which is cold and dry. Fire, which is hot and dry, shares the quality of dryness with earth and is the opposite of water, which is moist and cold. As the concept of tetrad became widely known, the humors started being linked to the seasons and the ages of human life as per a ninth-century treatise on the constitution of the world (Usher, 1989).

It was believed that the four humors in humans, which imitated the different elements, rose at different seasons and ruled at different ages of one's lifespan. Blood, which imitates the qualities of air, rises in the spring and rules mostly in childhood. Choler has the qualities of fire and rises in summer and rules in adolescence. Melancholy, which imitates the qualities of the earth, rises in autumn and rules in maturity. Finally, phlegm, which imitates the qualities of water, rises in winter and rules in old age. The idea that good health consists of a balance between the four elements was present from the beginning of Greek thought. Therefore, an excess of any one element was seen as a symptom of illness. The physician would treat these by trying to decrease the excess humor and bring the balance between the four humors. As we know, a person of intact health is a rarity. People eventually concluded that every person's constitution is dominated by one or another of the four humors.

Recognizing Your Child's Temperament Traits

Observation Techniques

Observing and identifying temperament traits requires study and deep theoretical knowledge about each temperament trait and your child. Understanding the two axes that govern temperament is essential to identifying temperament traits.

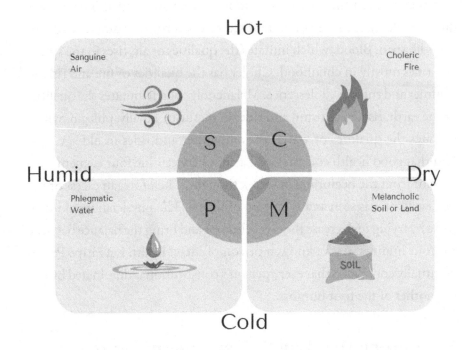

Hot

Sanguine
Air

Choleric
Fire

S   C

Humid

Dry

Phlegmatic
Water

P   M

Melancholic
Soil or Land

SOIL

Cold

Vertical Axis: The Hot-Cold Axis

The vertical axis is the hot-cold axis. Children whose behavior aligns with the vertical axis are of the temperament that falls under the hot-cold temperament.

Hot (Sanguine and Choleric)

The children who come under this axis are impulsive in nature. They react quickly, take action before thinking, and have quick and external reactions to what is happening at the moment. They talk excessively, often with expressive gestures and facial expressions. Speaking before taking the time to think about the subject is another of their traits. They think as they speak. Children are very extroverted and sociable. They get along with others easily and are the most comfortable in an external environment rather than doing silent tasks that need to be done alone.

Cold (Phlegmatic and Melancholic)

These children are more reserved and are more comfortable with their inner world. They are impacted by thoughts and emotions more than others, making them less enthusiastic about external activities or taking initiative. They'd rather spend their time doing quiet activities than participate in extroverted things. When faced with an idea or a problem, they need time to process the information before reacting or taking any action. They think a lot before making any decision or taking any action.

Assessing Which End of the Spectrum Your Child Is

Reaction to scolding:

When scolded, if the child reacts immediately, talks back, or argues, they are at the hot end of the axis. Whereas, if the child takes time to speak because they are thinking about what to say and making inner dialogues before taking action, they are at the cold end of the axis.

New people and the environment:

When exposed to new people or environments, children who show the desire to speak and express themselves are at the hot end of the axis. Conversely, suppose they listen to, observe, and analyze the person or environment. In that case, they are at the cold end of the vertical axis.

Horizontal Axis: The Humid and Dry Axis

Humid (Sanguine and Phlegmatic)

Children at this end of the axis are very adaptable. They are fluid, get involved with situations without much effort, and are good at collaborating with people. Since they are empathetic, they are considerate of the feelings and needs of others. Wet people can also maintain harmony in any relationship.

Dry (Choleric and Melancholic)

Children who are at the dry end of the axis are focused on principles and, therefore, are structured in their daily lives. They have good leadership skills and are motivated by their goals and ideas. They value their principles more than feelings and seek objectivity and clarity.

Assessing Which End of the Spectrum Your Child Is

Reaction to scolding:

When scolded, children on the dry end of the axis dwell on the incident. The scolding affects them so much that they remember it later.

On the other hand, children who are at the humid end of the axis let it go as soon as the scolding is over. They do not think about it later or take it to their heart.

New people and the environment:

Children at the axis's dry end internalize their impression of the new person or environment, prolonging it and giving it structure. Children at the humid end of the axis change and evolve their impression as they interact with the person or the new environment.

After assessment based on the child's behavior and actions using the above method, it can be determined which quadrant of the two axes the child's temperament falls under, as shown below. Hence, the child's temperament trait can be determined.

Hot and Dry Quadrant: Choleric
Hot and Humid: Sanguine
Dry and Cold: Melancholic
Cold and Humid: Phlegmatic

Supporting Diversity

Every child is unique, and so is their personality, based on their predominant temperament traits. Therefore, a tailored-for-all approach will not be effective for all children, especially those needing extra attention and a different approach than the norm. As parents and caretakers, we must become knowledgeable of the four temperament traits, recognize our child's dominant temperament trait, and change our parenting, teaching, and interaction styles accordingly. Every parent can create a thriving environment for their child by taking the time to understand their child's individual temperament trait and how it affects their thoughts and actions. Putting in the effort to do so will be rewarding in the sense that our child will feel heard and safe with us. It will ensure a stronger bond between the parent and the child, helping them open up more and share what's on their mind, which will help them grow into healthy adults.

ADHD vs. Temperament: Where Do We Draw the Line?

Overlap and Distinctions

The symptoms of ADHD and certain traits of temperaments look a lot alike. The terminology used to diagnose ADHD, like inattention, impulsivity, activity, and low task persistence, is also used to describe temperaments. A few empirical investigations have studied ADHD and temperament simultaneously, and research in the fields of ADHD and temperaments in children has been regarded as two separate bodies of knowledge.

The criteria for ADHD diagnosis in the US is based on the Diagnostic and Statistical Manual of Mental Disorders (DSM-IV-TR), which includes impairment within the areas of impulsivity, attention, and activity. ADHD inattentive, ADHD hyperactive-impulsive, and ADHD combined are the three subtypes. The presence of six or more symptoms in each group of inattention and hyperactivity present before the age of seven years is considered a clinical diagnosis. The symptoms must be seen in two or more settings, and the evidence of impairment in both social and academic functioning must be documented (American Psychiatric Association, 2000).

When observing the similarities and differences of the construct with ADHD, two complimentary perspectives of child temperament are particularly relevant. McClowry (1998) defined school-age temperament from a behavioral perspective as inborn dispositions that influence reactions to situations, especially those involving change or stress. McClowry (1995) also laid out four dimensions of school-age temperaments: negative reactivity, task persistence, activity, and approach/withdrawal. Based on the combinations of these four dimensions, McClowry (2002) also identified the temperament typologies. It was found that in her study of 883 participants, 14% of children had a "high maintenance" temperament profile. These children were also high in activity and negative reactivity and low in task persistence. The symptoms of this typology mirror that of ADHD.

Even though the theoretical overlap between ADHD and temperament is well established, only two studies have examined their empirical relationship. McIntosh & Cole-Love (1996) studied 70 male children ranging from 5 to 8 years old, of which 35 had ADHD and 35 didn't. They were from predominantly Anglo-American middle-class families in the Midwest U.S. Both parents and teachers rated them on the Temperament Assessment Battery for Children. It was concluded that children with ADHD exhibited temperaments that were high in activity and distractibility and low in persistence. The ones without ADHD were rated by the parents and teachers to be higher in task persistence and lower in activity and distractibility.

The second study was done by Bussing et al. (2003), who studied 200 male and female children ranging from eight to ten years old who screened positive on the Diagnostic Interview Schedule for the ADHD combined subtype. The children with ADHD combined subtype scored higher in activity and lower in task orientation than children in the non-ADHD group.

The conclusions from the studies of Bussing et al. (2003) and McIntosh and Cole-Love (1996) provide some empirical support for a relationship between the constructs of ADHD and temperament in children, but the questions regarding the distinctions between the two still remain. Because of the similarities between ADHD symptoms and child temperament traits, the diagnosis process is tricky. The children at the extreme end of a certain temperament trait, especially the hyperactive and impulsive children, have a chance of getting misdiagnosed as ADHD. Hence, a professional diagnosis is recommended over just caregiver observations.

Observable Signs of ADHD in Children

Core Symptoms

ADHD reveals itself through a combination of three core symptoms.

Inattention

This was once known as Attention Deficit Disorder (ADD). Children with predominantly inattentive ADHD have trouble focusing on a particular task, especially if they find the topic boring or repetitive. It is not that they are inattentive all the time; they will sometimes be hyperfocused on the tasks that interest them. They daydream a lot, too. They find it very difficult to complete a task they have started. They'll jump from one project, task, or hobby to the next without finishing the first one. Following instructions doesn't come easy as they skip necessary steps in procedures. As they get easily distracted by the environment, time management, organizing, and prioritizing tasks such as schoolwork is nearly impossible. Forgetfulness is a symptom of inattentive ADHD. They often lose or misplace items and forget even apparent things like bringing lunch, doing homework, and other things that might not take as much effort for a neurotypical child. Due to the lack of focus, they dislike and try to avoid tasks that require a lot of mental effort and may make careless mistakes, too. The most evident symptom is the trouble listening to people speak for a long time and staying on topic when speaking. If the topic of the conversation doesn't interest them, they'll tune out. This may cause them to lose friendships and lose opportunities to make genuine connections. Most times, inattentive ADHD goes unnoticed and undiagnosed until children start school and, in some cases, even into adulthood.

Hyperactive

The most commonly seen and easily recognized type in children is predominantly hyperactive/impulsive ADHD. The symptoms get more and more evident as children get older. In toddlers and preschoolers, the symptoms of hyperactive ADHD can be observed easily. Children with hyperactive ADHD are always on the go. They can't sit still and have to run around, jump on furniture, or climb a lot, even at inappropriate times. They don't enjoy quiet activities or hobbies like reading, painting, or group activities that require them to settle down and focus on the task. When made to sit down for a while in the classroom or elsewhere, you can see the child fidget and squirm a lot. They'll tap their feet, shake their legs, or their fingers will be drumming. They become extremely impatient to get up and move around. While they tend to speak a lot, sometimes even inappropriately, listening to a story or another person speak is hard. While some of these symptoms are common in any children of school-going age, in children with ADHD, you can see them more often. They seem unable to control themselves even at times that may be socially unacceptable.

Hyperactivity in teenagers shows itself in the form of restlessness and uneasiness. Teens with hyperactive ADHD also find it difficult to do group activities and quiet tasks. They have a quick temper and are talkative.

Impulsive

Children with impulsive ADHD lack patience and self-control. Asking them to be patient and wait a bit more for their turn may not work, as following such instructions is more complicated for them than for other children. They are not able to listen to someone speak without interrupting the conversation. They'll make tactless observations and ask irrelevant and off-topic questions during class. Without taking the time to think or solve the problem, they'll guess and blurt out the answers. Because of their impatient nature, children with impulsive ADHD are least bothered about respecting others' privacy—invading others' personal space and asking overly personal questions. They'll act without thinking and often end up doing inappropriate things at the wrong time, making others angry and hurting their feelings. This may result in others seeing the child as disrespectful. Having a grip on their emotions is tougher for impulsive children, leading to angry outbursts and temper tantrums. Impulsivity also leads to careless accidents like knocking things over and bumping into people or furniture while walking. It also makes them do risky things like climbing things and putting themselves in dangerous situations without stopping and thinking of the consequences of their actions.

Combination

This is the most common type of ADHD in children. They project symptoms of inattentiveness, hyperactivity, and impulsivity. A combination of these ADHD symptoms makes it evident for caretakers to notice that the child may have ADHD and consider clinical diagnosis.

Age-Appropriate Behaviors

Children are full of energy. Even after the parents get tired after playing with them, they still remain energetic enough to run a marathon. Some children are more active than others naturally, too. Just because children are super active and have short attention spans doesn't mean they have ADHD. Preschoolers naturally are less focused and more interested in jumping around than sitting still. The attention span in older children also depends on their interest level. It is not the occurrence of these symptoms but the frequency of it that determines a diagnosis.

The structure and function of certain parts of the brain of a child with ADHD are different than that of a neurotypical child. In a child with ADHD, the network of structures in the brain that puts you in a "daydream mode," called the Default Mode Network (DMN), is more active than in a neurotypical child. The chemical signals called neuro-transmitters, which pass messages between nerve cells in the brain, are also imbalanced in a child with ADHD. Because of these differences in brain functions and structure, children with ADHD find it harder to stay focused, manage their emotions, plan, and stay organized.

Often, children who struggle in school because of inattention and hyperactivity but do well at home and vice versa may be struggling with something other than ADHD. Therefore, just because a child is hyperactive or inattentive doesn't mean they have ADHD. It might just be their inborn nature or a reaction to some event.

When to Seek Help

As young children are, by nature, hyperactive and have short attention spans, it is hard to tell if the symptoms are ADHD or not. But if you see that problems with hyperactivity, inattention, or impulsivity occur more frequently and interfere with the child's daily life, even after applying the strategies and educational approaches you'll learn in this book, it's better to consult a doctor. If the child is not diagnosed with ADHD, the doctor might see these symptoms as signs of a language delay, learning disability, health issue, or a reaction to a possible traumatic life event. The doctor might suggest you take your child to a specialist in the field and get a proper diagnosis for your child's well-being.

The Power of Personalized Parenting

Parenting is an extremely challenging job, yet generation after generation, we continue to do it with love. Every new generation raises their children according to what they believe is the best parenting method based on what they have experienced and learned. With every generation, the parenting style changes. We have come a long way from the "spare the rod and spoil the child" era. Through different research and studies, we have realized that children misbehave for various reasons and are not simply misbehaving for no relevant reason. They are tiny individuals with their own struggles and need their parents' understanding and care to deal with them. The type of temperament trait of a child determines their characteristics. If they have ADHD, that will also make their and their family's lives more challenging when compared to other children without these characteristics.

A one-size-fits-all approach to parenting a child with ADHD and temperament differences will not be effective. They need their parents, caregivers, and educators to understand and consider their unique characteristics. A personalized parenting approach is crucial to tend to the special needs of children with ADHD and temperament differences. It involves learning about our child's strengths and how we can utilize the knowledge to modify our parenting style to benefit our child in a way that nourishes their best abilities to mitigate their daily struggles and succeed in academics and other fields.

A personalized parenting approach will help your child with their daily struggles by making them capable of managing and dealing with them. It will also positively affect your relationship with your child. Your child will notice that you are putting in extra effort for them, and the positive changes in their life will make them happy and strengthen your relationship. Your tailored parenting style will eventually bring your child closer to you, making them feel connected and ready to open up to you more. Your child will know that mommy and daddy understand them and are there for them.

Observing your child for some time will give an insight into what they are good at and what needs extra attention. Observe their learning styles, socialization with others, and interactions with their surroundings, and talk to them about their likes and dislikes and if there is anything they would like you to do or help them with. Be there for them and adapt your ways to meet their evolving needs as they grow and learn more. When you are helping your child, make sure that you are not completely taking over. Let them handle things on their own with your guidance. If your child is a visual learner, help them stick their mathematics formulas and notes on their study space wall. If they learn better by listening, recite their notes for them or encourage them to read aloud while studying. If your child is hyperactive, find ways to channel that energy into healthy activities like an hour at the park or joining sports or dance classes. Focus on enhancing their strengths and making them stronger where their weaknesses lie.

Understanding Your Child's World

Everyone perceives the world around them differently. However, children with ADHD and temperament differences experience hugely different things from any other child who does not have these characteristics. Their world is constantly changing, and they struggle to focus on one thing because something new and exciting catches their eye. Their world is busy and loud, and so is their mind. We need to understand that they get distracted and lose interest because of how their brains are wired. They often get labeled as difficult.

These children need not punishment but discipline, a little empathy and understanding. As parents, we must first work our patience and behavior to help our children. We cannot lash out at them when they repeat the same behavior repeatedly. They really don't mean to; they do it unintentionally. Children with ADHD often forget things and have difficulty following a series of instructions. There are things that these children struggle with that other kids don't. The best way to approach this behavior is to let your child know you are there to support and help them. Make them feel seen and understood. Remind them of the important things several times, give them instructions individually, and help them stay organized. Encourage your child to share their thoughts and feelings. Talk to them about your day and ask them about theirs. Make sure your home is a peaceful, safe space supporting your child's needs and promoting a sense of belonging.

Chapter 2: Tools for Temperament Assessment

Understanding the temperaments of our family members, especially our daughter, has been crucial in fostering our growth and well-being. By identifying our unique temperament, we've tailored our parenting approach and family relationship to meet our needs and strengths. Recognizing this has allowed us to provide better support, create a more harmonious home environment, and reeducate ourselves in ways that align with personal development. This personalized approach has strengthened our relationships and helped us thrive in all areas of our lives.

Additionally, getting to know our extended family members and friends' temperaments feels like having a superpower that enhances our understanding and fosters greater empathy. By recognizing each person's unique traits and preferences, we gain valuable insights into their behaviors and needs, which helps us respond with more compassion and support. This deeper awareness empowers us to communicate more effectively, resolve conflicts more efficiently, and build stronger, more harmonious relationships within our family.

Let's delve into the world of temperaments.

Introducing Temperament Assessment Tools

Understanding your temperament is crucial for effective parenting because it allows you to tailor your approach to education and discipline to align with your natural tendencies. For instance, a choleric parent might need to be mindful of their assertive style and find balance. In contrast, a sanguine parent might benefit from structuring routines to help manage enthusiasm and maintain consistency. Recognizing your temperament helps identify your strengths and areas for improvement, enabling you to create a supportive and nurturing environment that plays to your strengths while addressing potential challenges.

Equally important is understanding your child's temperament, as it provides insight into their needs, preferences, and behavioral tendencies. A child with a melancholic temperament might require more reassurance and structured guidance. In contrast, a sanguine child may thrive with more flexibility and social interaction. By aligning your parenting strategies with your child's temperament, you can better address their emotional needs, foster their development, and build a more harmonious relationship. This personalized approach helps their development and reduces conflicts to establish a positive and efficient learning environment.

Here are three suggestions for simple temperament tests available online that can help you identify your own and your child's temperament.

   1. **Four Temperaments Test by Dr. Robert W. Long**

   ○ **Link:** Four Temperaments Test

   ○ **Description:** This test is specifically designed to evaluate the four classical temperaments. It provides insights into which of the four temperaments is most dominant in your personality.

27

2. **The Classical Temperament Test**

   ○ **Link:** Classical Temperament Test

   ○ **Description:** This test assesses the balance of the four classical temperaments in your personality. It's a straightforward quiz that should give you a clear idea of your dominant temperament.

3. **HITOSTAT Temperaments Test**

   ○ **Link:** Temperaments Test

   ○ **Description:** This test evaluates your personality based on the four temperaments framework and provides a comprehensive report on your temperament profile.

These tests should help you understand your temperament.

Other assessment tools vary from questionnaires, observation checklists, interviews, and performance-based tasks to rating scales.

Choosing the right tool of assessment for your child is essential. Consider your child's age, ease of use, what results you expect from this assessment, and what you need to assess to help your child. Also, make sure that the particular assessment test is valid and reliable.

These tests are conducted to detect and understand our child's and our own temperament traits. Gaining knowledge about our strengths and weaknesses will help us tailor our approach to parenting and guide and empower our children to a better life.

The Airy Sanguine

Children with a sanguine temperament are always curious. Their interest in something is quickly turned on, and they are eager to know more. They are very adventurous and outgoing and love company. Being the center of attention is something they love, which may end up disrupting the class or atmosphere at home. Though they have difficulty obeying and understanding their parents and teachers, they want to please them. They tend to shy away from hard, continuous effort and find it challenging to stick to the same activity for some time, like a game or learning something because their attention is scattered. Though they are lazy when it comes to studying and need help achieving depth in studying, they learn quickly but may need help memorizing. They are very attuned to the five senses. As they are very expressive, you can see the rapid fluctuation of their moods and emotions on their face. They can go from crying to laughing in the blink of an eye and vice-versa. Patience is not their strong suit; they want everything to happen immediately. Waiting for something is very difficult for them. Scolding sanguine children has little effect on them as it goes in one ear and out the other. As soon as the scolding ends, they'll move on to their next task without dwelling on what the parent said. But they are also the most apologetic ones. They repent promptly and truly but often make the same mistake again.

They can have a delay in mastering speech, and it will make the child very irritable. They will get angry and frustrated because they cannot express themselves well with words. They may cry, hit, or throw themselves on the floor in their frustration to make the other person understand their need. This can be as difficult for the parent as it is for the child. However, rather than being disheartened, the parents should act calmly and try to soothe the child first. Try to communicate with them with patience.

Since sanguine children try to please everyone, they give up on their beliefs and try to fit other people's perspectives. This can lead to an identity crisis later on in life. Because of their people-pleasing nature, they can be easily influenced. Therefore, a sense of justice and morality should be taught early to avoid getting involved in bad company.

Strengths

Sanguine people live in the moment without dwelling on the past or worrying about the future. They are good-hearted, compassionate, generous, friendly, cheerful, and optimistic. They feel and express themselves openly and are not stubborn, nor do they hold grudges. Making friends, interacting, and communicating well are some of their strong suits. Because of this trait, they are also expansive in terms of relationships. They are also very adventurous and have a creative side to them. They are particular about details and very attentive to their appearance.

Weaknesses

They speak before thinking and sometimes cause hurt to others, often apologizing a lot. They are also superficial, prone to exaggeration, and mock others for fun. Sanguine people immediately think that they have understood something and assimilate without depth. Difficulty retaining information, elaborating on things, understanding, and obeying parents are drawbacks of this temperament.

There are three types of sanguine temperaments:

Humid Over Hot (Breeze)

They love socializing and doing fun activities. They often end up talking too much and in more detail than needed. As they are very generous, they love to serve others. As decision-making comes from heat, which is low in them, they tend to need more time to decide. Also, they tend to have attention deficits and need help organizing and making wise choices. Therefore, these children need much help from their parents in their practical lives. They'll need a little more aid with their homework, which their parents must help until they age.

Hot Over Humid (Hurricane)

This is the most outgoing temperament and is often considered rebellious. They like pushing boundaries, searching for new ideas, and desiring freedom. Therefore, they like to act more than they think or articulate. They talk too much and want to be a part of things that their parents or adults do. They are quick to understand the situation and are considered intelligent. Even though they have the upper hand in grasping things, they don't delve into anything and need help retaining the information received.

Hot Over Humid With Dry Input (Strong Wind)

Children with this type of air temperament are the most practical type of all. They don't talk too much. Their words and intellect are directed toward more meaningful things. They are dedicated, productive, and are born leaders. The dryness in the hot over humid with dry input temperament drives action; hence, they have practical intelligence and find solutions to problems rather than frowning about them. Even with this level of intellect, these children don't put as much effort into their studies as they can and, therefore, do initially well, but it may not be constant. They know their abilities and how far they can go but fear they may falter. They have high mood swings and become insecure teenagers as they grow up.

The Sizzling Choleric

Choleric children are decisive and stubborn. They are hard workers and strive to get better every time. They like challenges and keep going until they succeed. But they also get easily irritated, angry, and needy, especially when things don't go their way. Being a leader comes naturally to them. They have a lot of energy and show affection with blows and pushing, which might sometimes be annoying. Admitting that they were wrong and apologizing does not come easy to them. Often, their words and actions may be inconsiderate of the feelings of others.

Suppose choleric children are brought up by their parents without an attentive upbringing. In that case, it will lead to dangerous personality traits in adolescence and adulthood. They become more resistant and reckless, not recognizing authority or asking for help even when desperate. If these children are punished a lot for every little mistake, they'll try to hide things from their parents for fear of being punished. They'll start to lie and manipulate to escape being scolded, punished, or just to be seen as a good child. They'll rebel in adolescence if their parents don't believe in them and don't recognize and support what they can do.

Strengths

Choleric children are confident leaders who understand situations well. They can handle any situation with their quick thinking and practical solutions. They are outgoing and express their ideas and words without hesitation. They are intelligent, determined, competitive, and strong-willed. They see everything in a positive light, and these qualities make them excellent leaders.

Weaknesses

Choleric children's dominant, stubborn, and impatient nature and non-willingness to listen can be challenging. They are proud and disdain those with less talent, sometimes making them harsh and insensitive. They can be excessively ambitious, which may hurt their lives and the lives of those around them.

There are three types of choleric temperaments:

Dry Over Hot (Spark)

Dry on hot choleric people are more overbearing, critical, and judgmental. Deep anger, resentment, and arrogance can make them antisocial and troublemakers. Challenges and opportunities drive them. They are productive because of their discipline and meticulous and strategic approach to the things they do. Forgiving someone is hard for them because of their proud and obstinate nature. Children get physical quickly and cause trouble in school and at home. Even though they seem irritable at times, these people are very ethical and honest.

Hot Over Dry (Flame)

They are born leaders and exercise their authority with elegance and strength. They have a clear perception of what they need and don't take into account other people's opinions. They are less controlling of others and are compassionate. Children feel a sense of protection towards their younger siblings and friends. They know what they need and like to start new hobbies or tasks and have the required focus to complete them. They are also impatient, get angry quickly, and hold onto resentment. Parents of these children should provide a leadership model for them because they look up to their parents as the ones leading them and learn from them.

Hot Over Dry With Humid Input (Ember)

The humid input in children's hot over dry temperament gives them the sensitivity to compassion toward others. It makes them fair and just. They are good, flexible leaders who consider what others have to say and act based on what is right and just. They are creative, sensitive, and charismatic while remaining assertive. They are very good at adapting to the environment they are in. They always try to be sympathetic to others but can't because of their dryness. Children with this temperament type need parents and teachers who exert their authority. If not, they will look for it elsewhere and get in trouble.

The Organic Melancholy

Melancholic children behave very well in their early years without troubling their parents. They are slow and passive and love routines. They are friendly and love to play with everyone but will have only a handful of friends. They are methodical perfectionists and don't like unnecessary talking. Children with a melancholic temperament are closer to their parents; they love spending time with them. They seldom fight with other children and won't react immediately when reprimanded for something.

Since melancholic children are mostly silent and don't disobey or cause much trouble, parents tend to be the talkative ones. When the child occasionally makes some mistake, if the parents blame them unreasonably, the child will get distant and start to dislike the parents. Since they have always been good, obedient children, when the parents don't try to understand or listen to them, they feel it is unfair and can lead to disheartenment. If there were physical punishments, the child will become aggressive and disconnected from the family when they become teens. It will make them bitter, pessimistic, sad, and distant. Therefore, parents should be observant and considerate by trying to understand the child before blaming them or punishing them. Try to strengthen the bond so they can rely on you in difficult times. They may not seem to have trouble, but that is not always the case.

Strengths

They value everything noble, like truth, justice, and beauty. They persevere by abiding by their principles even when the going gets tough. Choleric children are very obedient, sensitive, and compassionate. They are intelligent with an aptitude for science and a love for the arts. If educated well, they'll reach great heights professionally. Organization and attention to detail are their strong suits and help them in school and at home. They like solitude and will align with their environment without disturbing it. When things go wrong, they tend toward self-denial. Parents should pay close attention to their children with melancholic temperaments and help them in complex situations.

Weaknesses

Melancholic children are often seen as shy, but this is not true. They are not shy at all. Instead, they like the company of only a few and don't feel the need to express themselves at all times. They are perfectionists and, therefore, end up judging others for not being one. When it comes to making a decision, they are not very quick. Because of their fear of failure, they'll weigh every pro and con and try to make the most ideal decision or give in to other people's decisions. Since they like solitude, sometimes they isolate themselves even in a crowd. The child may be in a playground full of children but will not approach anyone and play all alone. They don't initiate friendships, and when they find someone, even then, the relationship building is very slow. This mindset hinders friendships or makes them outcasts among other children. It is also difficult for them to forgive the ones who hurt them.

There are three types of melancholy temperaments:

Dry Over Cold (Rock)

This type of melancholic child is a persevering, determined leader with the potential for greatness. Their leadership qualities make them a strong support for others. They are meticulous perfectionists and want everything to go their way. As much as they are perfectionists, they are also the most prominent critics of themselves. Even after putting in their best efforts, they'll still need more. They are seen as selfish and controlling, with a lack of trust when interacting and working with others.

Cold Over Dry (Soil)

When they grow up, these children tend to become hoarders because of their attachment to material things and inability to get rid of them. They put so much emotional meaning to things like the toys they own that it dominates over what's actually meaningful in life. They are secure, foresighted, and organized but not perfectionists. They are sociable but don't make friends easily and are easy to forgive others. Even though they are sociable, they are not interested in other people's lives and don't deepen their friendships, maintaining a fine balance. An organized environment helps them be more cordial and calm, which might also help with their often pessimistic mind.

Cold Over Dry with Humid Input (Wet Soil)

These types of melancholic children have an explosive component to them. They also like to accumulate things and, in this case, relationships too, and attach more meaning to them than they mean. Like things, they want more human relationships, like friends and family. They expect more from them and end up disappointed and frustrated. They have great ambitions, which are more significant than anyone they know, like living an entirely different life, becoming the leader who commands, and having more abilities. Still, when they fail, they see themselves as inferior to others and get disappointed. These children need good guidance so they don't give up and are led on the right track to maximize their potential.

The Moldable Phlegmatic

Phlegmatic children are rule-abiding, quiet, obedient kids. When reprimanded, they don't understand the scolding but will stop what they are doing and change the activity. Sharing toys and other stuff comes easily to them. They like to play with other children and don't mind losing in games. They enjoy books and movies and usually have stable behavior, hardly ever throwing tantrums.

Since they are very good at hiding their feelings, it is tricky for the parents to know what is happening with the child. But without the guidance and leadership of strong parents, they can be led astray by bad company. They are easily influenced if they are in a bad environment. As parents, you will need to push them to help them with their self-improvement; they are incapable of self-motivation because they tended towards idleness and demotivation. Punishments and even rewards only give them temporary motivation, and they'll need constant support from their parents to thrive. When it comes to making a decision or persevering at a task they are already doing, they can become hesitant, indecisive, and fearful. Therefore, parents have an essential role in helping their phlegmatic children reach their potential and grow up to become adults capable of dealing with the world.

Strengths

Phlegmatic children are observers who patiently listen to others and are empathetic. They keep calm even under pressure, moving away from conflicts and bad company and looking for good friends. They hate confrontation and try to stay away from it if possible. When there is a goal they are trying to achieve, like studying for a test, they become committed, constant, and persevering. Whatever they do, they are always orderly, detailed, clear, and concise about it. If intellectually talented, they have the willpower and potential to become geniuses. They are loyal and reliable friends but very reserved and sensitive at the same time. Tolerance is a trait they possess; as a result, they hardly ever get angry or feel insulted. No one can belittle them and hope they feel awful. They are stronger than that.

Weaknesses

Phlegmatic children are passive and slow to act. They lack spontaneity and enthusiasm, which can often make them look lazy. They don't have any big goals and are not interested in challenges; they're happy as they are. When they are slow to act, like answering a question in class, it signals their lack of interest, and they could get labeled as slow learners.

There are three types of phlegmatic temperaments:

Humid Over Cold (Steam)

This is the phlegmatic type with its classic traits. They are more sensitive and intuitive than the others. Their empathy gives them the advantage of understanding others well, which means they try to please others. When this type of phlegmatic child is asked to do something, they listen well and want to obey. Still, when it comes to action, they somehow cannot perform the task, making them misinterpreted as disobedient. They have great recollections of things but are poor at expressing them well.

Cold Over Humid (Water)

Cold over humid phlegmatic children can be mistaken for choleric children because of similar traits like impulsivity and reactivity. But unlike choleric people, they think before they act. They are thinkers and great at introspection. They are braver than the other phlegmatic children and deeply understand things, situations, and people. They can also be vindictive and, at times, spiteful.

Cold Over Humid With Dry Input (Ice)

This type of phlegmatic child can be described as a child with an adult nature. They are introspective, affectionate, considerate of others' well-being, and try not to create conflicts or get involved. They need stability, and even though they are emotional, they are good at keeping it detached from other aspects of their life. Emotional comfort is important, and material stability makes them feel secure.

Summary of the 3 types within each main temperament

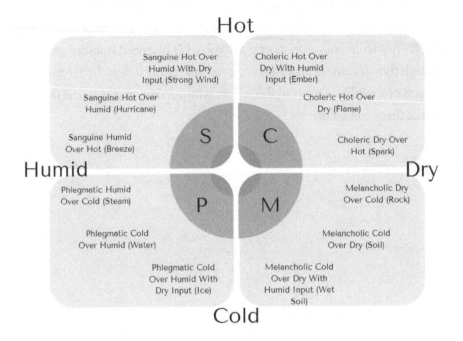

Tailoring Your Parenting Approach to Temperament

Understanding your child's temperament helps in knowing how the child reacts to and relates to specific situations and people around them. Their actions are not intentional, just a result of their temperament. As much as it is crucial to recognize your child's temperamental traits, it is also essential to know your own. The way the parent reacts and responds to the child and their parenting approach is highly influenced by their own temperament type. Observing your thoughts, reactions, and words will give insight into your temperament, which will eventually help change your parenting style to best suit your child's needs rather than your instincts. The way that children get along with others is influenced by not just their temperament or personality but also by their parents' parenting style.

A study by Thomas and Chess on 141 infants, called the "New York Longitudinal Study," started in 1956 and continued for several decades until the children reached adolescence and adulthood (Thomas & Chess, 1977). The study involved direct observations and interviews with the parents of the child subjects. After investigating their personality and temperaments, the team identified and rated nine different qualities associated with personality and temperament. The nine characteristics that were found to be reliably scorable on a three-point system were:

- Activity level: How much fidgeting, jumping, running around, and other physical activity does the child engage in daily.

- Rhythmicity: If there is any regular pattern for basic physical functions such as eating, sleeping, and bowel movement.

- Response to a new object or person: Their first response to new situations, like a change in routine, meeting new people, or a new environment. Observations were done to see if they adapted quickly or withdrew.

- Adaptability: How well they adapted to new environments, people, food, or routines.

- Sensory threshold: How quickly they respond to stimuli and if they respond to the slightest stimuli or require intense amounts to react.

- Intensity of response: The energy level with which a child responds to a positive or negative situation.

- Mood: The general mood of the child. The child is generally happy or cranky, friendly or unfriendly.

- Distractibility: When doing something, do they get distracted by their environment, such as light, sound, or movements around them?

- Attention span: How long the child can focus and stay on the task they are doing.

When the researchers analyzed these behaviors, some of them seemed to cluster together, forming three general types of temperament (Thomas & Chess, 1977):

- The easy children: About 40 percent of the 141 children were characterized under this group. These children were generally happy and easily adapted to new situations, routines, and people. When they got older, they adapted well to school and participated in activities. They mostly abided by the rules, causing little to no trouble.

- The difficult children: As infants, these children were slower to adapt to new foods and routines, with irregular feeding and sleeping, and tended to cry a lot. As they got older, they seemed to overreact and took time to adapt to new environments. They also showed violent tantrums, loud laughter, and cries. The parents need to put in extra effort to raise these children—ten percent of the sampled children of this group.

- The slow-to-warm-up children: Fifteen percent of the children studied were in the "slow-to-warm-up" category. They had relatively low activity levels and were slow to adapt to new things. They did not smile and responded to situations with less intensity.

From this study, Thomas and Chess observed that an adult's personality was not only dependent on their childhood temperament but also a combination of that temperament and the environment they were brought up in, including their parenting style.

Therefore, in 1977, Thomas and Chess founded a concept called "Goodness of Fit," which encompasses the match between the child's needs and the parent's parenting style. This concept proposes that when the child's characteristics fit their environment's demands, it will result in adaptive outcomes (Thomas & Chess, 1977). This theory has been proven to be an essential aspect of children's healthy social and emotional development. The "Goodness of Fit" concept, or adapting your parenting style according to your child's temperament, does not mean avoiding conflict. With labor, children can reach their developmental milestones (Thomas & Chess, 1977). For a good fit, your expectations from your child should align with the child's age, temperament type, skills, and abilities (Ostergren, 1997). This way, they won't feel like they have failed when they cannot meet your expectations, and you, as the parent, will be doing the best for your child. You can also help them understand their temperament and how reactions act against them or help them in various situations. Help them share the uniqueness in their traits with their teachers and friends so they can understand each other better. This will lead to a healthy parent-child relationship and promote the child's physical and emotional growth and development.

Celebrating Your Child's Strengths

Identifying Strengths and Weaknesses

Every child is different. Even your own two children are two entirely different human beings. So, their strengths and weaknesses will differ. What one is good at, the other might find difficult. Therefore, as parents, we must observe and discover our children's strengths and weaknesses to help them and raise them well. A good observation of your child's response and reactions to things and situations in their daily life will give you a context of what they are good at and struggle with. Observe them as they play with other children, study, do basic things like eating and putting on clothes by themselves, and how they interact with you, their teachers, and their peers. Soon, you will see some distinguished characters and patterns in their behavior. Their temperament trait and your observations will give you a picture of your child's personality and their strengths and weaknesses. Once you have figured them out, you can help them with things they struggle with in a way that helps them get better at it. With the things that they are good at, you can help them by creating an environment at home that will nourish their skills.

It is essential to focus on our children's achievements and strengths. Parents often get fixated on things going wrong, like bad grades, disobedience, talking too much in class, and tantrums, so their achievements get overshadowed and ignored. As much as condemning lousy behavior is necessary for building character in children, scolding them for what they are doing wrong and not congratulating and supporting them in their successes leads to an imbalance. The child will cultivate resentment and become distant from the parent. They will feel like all their efforts are being ignored and think their parents do not see their potential and only see them as failures. Therefore, praising them when they succeed, appreciating their efforts, and showing them support with words are necessary to build their self-esteem. This will build their confidence and help them put their best efforts into things. They will try harder, and in the future, they will gain the confidence to face the world.

Practical Activities

Based on their strengths, parents can indulge their children in some practical activities that will help them explore and develop their strengths further. Extrovert children who love physical activities can be trained for sports they may like, take gymnastics classes, or participate in group work-

44

outs that will help them showcase their talents and develop them further. Children who are more introverted and like silent activities can indulge in activities like painting, writing, reading, singing, chess, or other activities that align with their strengths. They can participate in competitions of their choice, which will help them boost their confidence and self-esteem.

Identifying and celebrating your children's strengths and weaknesses is essential. It will enable you to help them further develop their talents, eventually find their passion, and build their lives.

Addressing Challenges with Compassion and Strategy

Parents often get triggered by their children's bad behavior and jump to action before even thinking about the cause of that behavior. We may scold and punish them without showing patience to hear their side of the story. Their actions and reactions are rooted in their temperament type and the situations they get involved in. They feel wronged if we don't consider their struggle before punishing them. We all want to raise children into physically and mentally healthy adults. In that case, it is necessary to look beyond the surface behaviors and understand the underlying causes of their behaviors. Knowing their temperament type is a huge help in understanding the child's behavior. As discussed earlier, you can find out which temperament type your child falls under, giving you a perspective on how they see and respond to the world. Different temperament types react differently in the same situations. If you can understand the root cause, you can help your child improve their behaviors and deal with the situation better.

Compassionate communication is the key to understanding your child's point of view. No amount of scolding or punishment will give the same result as building a solid relationship with your child. Open and loving conversations and interactions are the key to reaching them. Sit them down and talk to them when they are struggling. Ask them about their day and be interested in their life. Get involved with their school activities, play with them, and do things together like shopping, doing chores, or playing. When there is an issue at home or school, listen to them and solve the problem together. Find out what they are upset about and struggling with, and sort it out together. Discuss with them how they can use their strengths to face their challenges. Talk to them and work with them to find the root cause of their struggles. Let them know that they can overcome their struggles and that you are there for them. Avoid only looking at negative behaviors and focus on their good deeds. Appreciate them, show them you see their effort, and support them wholeheartedly. When punishing them for bad behavior, have a calm, compassionate talk with them to make them understand what they did wrong and why they are being punished. Also, discuss with them how they can improve and do better next time. Give them the space to reflect on their behavior and a chance to improve. This will bring your child closer to you; they will feel safe enough to reach out to you if needed, and you will understand them and their actions better. They will be less rebellious and more understanding when they know that you will be there for them no matter what.

The Impact of Temperament on Learning Styles

Each child is unique, and their temperament type makes them even more diverse than each other. Their temperamental trait makes them respond and react to situations differently. The same is the case when it comes to learning. Not all children learn the same way. They need different educational approaches to help them understand and develop. Their temperament traits influence their preferred learning styles and strategies. Academic achievement is related to temperament traits. In a school environment, during class, the child will have to settle down, focus their attention and energy on the class, and persist even if the class is long. They are not particularly interested in the subject. Task orientation is the most important temperament dimension affecting a child's academic success. Task orientation is related to the child's activity level, persistence, and distractibility. Therefore, a child who can moderate their physical activity appropriately, ignore distractions, and maintain their focus on the task will be an academic achiever. In contrast, other children who struggle with it will not be able to do well academically.

Many achievement and behavior problems children face in schools are caused by their temperament not aligning with their school environment and their teacher's temperament type. A change in the classroom environment, a teacher who understands the child's unique needs, and making the class as distraction-free as possible will help a lot in improving their academic success. Engage the child in activities that strengthen their abilities and support them as they learn new skills and adapt to the learning environment.

Talk with your child's teachers and learn about their behavior in class. Collaborate with the teacher to support your child's learning needs according to their temperament type. Discuss your child's strengths, weaknesses, and choice of learning method with them. The teacher and the parent should be on the same page regarding the child's education.

In a homeschool environment, the power of customized education becomes even more pronounced, as parents have the unique opportunity to tailor their teaching methods to perfectly align with their child's temperament and learning style. Unlike traditional school settings, homeschooling allows for a highly personalized approach, where parents can adjust the pace, environment, and content of lessons to meet their child's specific needs. Parents can significantly enhance their child's academic success and overall well-being by creating a learning environment that minimizes distractions and caters to the child's strengths and weaknesses.

Homeschooling also facilitates a deeper understanding between parent and child, enabling a more intuitive and responsive teaching strategy. Parents can engage their children in activities that bolster their academic skills and nurture their personal interests and passions. This individualized approach ensures that the child is learning effectively, motivated, and engaged. Open communication between parents and children about learning preferences and challenges allows for continuous adjustment and improvement in the educational experience. Ultimately, the flexibility of homeschooling empowers parents to craft an education plan uniquely suited to their child, fostering an environment where they can thrive academically and emotionally.

Strategies for Every Temperament

Different strategies can be followed depending on the child's temperament trait.

Activity Level

Hot-axis children (Sanguine & Choleric) have a lot of energy. Give them opportunities for movement, like regular exercise and active outside time, or they will start misbehaving. Fast-action sports and activities will help channel their energy effectively. If possible, give them periodic breaks between the studies or table activities. During the night, follow a daily wind-down ritual for a good sleep.

Cold-axis children (Phlegmatic & Melancholic) are less active and need a push to take action. Encourage them to exercise daily and restrict TV time and other passive entertainment. Give them extra time to wake up in the morning, as they need time to process and take the next step.

Sensitivity

Hot-axis children with high sensitivity see and feel everything with intensity. They need regular quiet time and adequate space. They get easily stimulated, so avoid spending too much time in crowded and noisy places. You can help your child gain control over unnecessary stimulation by asking them questions like if they need some quiet time and what would make them calm down and take care of themselves.

Cold-axis children with low sensitivity have a high tolerance for stimulation, so they might be insensitive to others. Encourage them to pay close attention to their surroundings. Teach them patience and make them understand that other's experiences may be different from theirs.

Regular or Irregular

Cold-axis children who are regular in their routines love patterns, and any change or disruption can upset them. To avoid this, mix up their routines occasionally to help them learn to adapt.

Hot-axis children, especially sanguine, with irregularity, are spontaneous, which may not be good, especially if you want them to follow a plan. Set up routines that allow flexibility while also creating a structure. Help them set goals and achieve them.

First Response to New Situations

Hot-axis children who quickly adapt to a new environment or person are impulsive and can be accident-prone. Help them think before jumping to action and encourage them to slow down and be considerate of others.

Cold-axis children with low adaptability need a lot of patience. Give them ample time for transitions and remind them before any changes.

Persistence and Frustration Tolerance

A child with low persistence and high frustration will give up easily. They need their parents' encouragement and support. Break down activities into small sections and gradually increase difficulty levels to help them adapt.

Highly persistent children can be challenging. Put down the rules and stick by them. Teach your child negotiation skills and give them choices.

Distractibility

The attention span of highly distracted children is deficient. They continuously jump from one thing to the next. Give one instruction at a time and teach them to focus on one thing at a time.

Try to be flexible and accommodate your child's needs per their temperament traits. Approaching parenting with the knowledge of your child's temperament type and traits will bring you closer to your child and help them succeed in every field.

Beyond Labels: Overcoming the Weaknesses

Labeling a child is not the right approach to raising capable adults. Instead of labeling them by their temperaments or ADHD diagnosis, parents and teachers should focus on viewing the child as unique and tend to their overall development.

Holistic View of the Child

Early childhood education should not only be about academics. The overall development of the child is essential. Taking a holistic approach to teaching is the best way to do so. Holistic education focuses on all aspects of a child's growth, including physical, mental, emotional, intellectual, and social growth. It focuses on the child's overall well-being and not just academics. Holistic development consists of three processes. Firstly, the biological process is how babies physically transform from children to adults. It involves physical growth and brain development. Secondly, the cognitive process is how children's thinking, intelligence and language skills develop from simple to complex. Lastly, the social-economic process is how the child's personality, emotions, and interpersonal connections grow from childish to mature. These three interconnected processes are equally important for a child's healthy growth. Parents should be aware of every phase of a child's growth, including their developmental milestones during prenatal, infancy, toddlerhood, early childhood, middle, and late childhood. At the same time, it must be kept in mind that not every child reaches the milestones simultaneously. A holistic approach to education and development will cater to every aspect of the child's growth, making them physically, mentally, and emotionally healthy.

Avoiding Stigma and Empowering Your Child

Every child expresses themselves differently. Shaming them for their actions is not the right approach to changing their behaviors. Comparing your child to their friends and siblings because of their differences leaves a mark on their hearts. It will complicate things, and you become more distant from your child. Talking about their weaknesses in a public situation will hurt and negatively impact them. Avoid embarrassing them or comparing them to others. A parent should be the one they lean on, giving them the love and courage to work on their strengths. Don't avoid their weaknesses, but help them overcome the hurdles together. Don't let their failures define them. Your children are much more than their actions, and you are the one who should tell them that.

Empower your child with the right tools to persevere no matter how hard the road gets. When the child's behavior is unacceptable or needs guidance, sit with them and have a conversation. Discuss what went wrong and how they can improve and do things differently. Show them how they can work on their strong suits to improve. Empowering your child will ensure they are capable enough for the adult world when they are older.

Triumphs Over Temperament and ADHD Challenges

It is very common for parents to assume that their children have an attention deficit or hyperactivity when they encounter the diagnostic criteria for the disorder. However, external factors like diet, sleep, routine, and physical activity that are part of the child's daily life and directly impact their development should be considered.

Understanding each child's natural strengths and weaknesses is the first step to successful parenting. This is followed by making fundamental changes in daily routines and then applying strategies that help change behavior.

An example of a child who would be diagnosed with attention deficit disorder if she were in school is our own 9-year-old daughter. A typical hot and humid sanguine, we joke that she is our butterfly because she always seems to fly from flower to flower. From a very young age, we noticed that she was easily distracted by stimuli unrelated to what she was doing, had difficulty organizing herself, resisted activities that required a lot of mental effort and couldn't follow two or three commands given at the same time.

We quickly recognized our daughter's deficits and knew we would have to be very present in the early years of her moral and intellectual development if we wanted her to overcome her weaknesses and gain her full potential.

After changing her essential habits, we began to study her temperament more closely. Then, we understood her natural, intrinsic reactions and began to nip them in the bud. That's right; we must consider that our weaknesses are part of our nature, which we don't want to feed. If you stop giving a plant the nutrients it needs, it will die, right? It's the same with temperaments: discover the weakness and stop nurturing that disposition.

One of the biggest challenges this type of sanguine generally has is following instructions. As parents, we were very frustrated and often thought she didn't want to obey. For example, when asked to brush her teeth, make her bed, and change her clothes after breakfast, she usually only did the first task (brushing her teeth). The next thing we knew, she was in her room playing. So one of us would come in and draw her attention, and she'd say, "Sorry, I forgot, Mom," and immediately start making the bed, but she wouldn't change her clothes. We changed things a bit when we realized that this difficulty was part of her nature and that she needed to be educated to act differently. We began to give her one instruction at a time to help her retain the information. So the commands went like this: We'd ask her to brush her teeth and come back. She'd do it and come back, "That's it, Mom, I've brushed my teeth!" Then we'd ask her to tidy her room and come back, and so on. One command at a time, that's how it went for a long time, then we increased it to two commands. Soon after, we could give her three instructions: brush her teeth, make her bed, and change her clothes. But she still leaves her pajamas on the bed and the bathroom sink soaking wet. The details don't stick easily in this type of sanguine, so parents must keep working until they achieve.

One strategy that really helps us to succeed against our daughter's natural weaknesses is Bible stories. We use characters who have faced the same difficulties as examples of overcoming and how much God can do for us when we place our weaknesses in His care.

A few years ago, we worked with a family whose child was choleric, hot over dry with a wet input. The melancholic mother had high expectations of her son's formal education. Like any mother, she wanted to do her best with homeschooling. However, there was a visible imbalance in the child's essential habits, with practically all his autonomy compromised, from sleeping to eating and even basic personal hygiene routines. In short, we spent a few weeks trying to align this part before entering the academic educational process, and only then did we succeed with our little warrior who loved to challenge his parents and caregivers.

When this mother came to us, her main complaint was that she couldn't do any activity with her son. He was always agitated, had difficulty sitting down to do an activity to the end, and couldn't concentrate on reading aloud or even playing quietly. He was always jumping, climbing, or, in other words, at full steam all the time.

In the first conversation, we saw the need to reform the routine. We changed the boy's diet and sleep routine, and that alone helped immensely in the change. He cut carbs and sugar. He also needed to learn to sleep alone and thus have nights of uninterrupted sleep. Once this was done, we established a routine, and before long, this mother was overjoyed that there were no more fights over taking a bath; her son sat down to listen to a story, and she was able to carry out homeschool activities with him. In short, he was an apparently hyperactive child. Still, he fed his weaknesses so much that his strengths were compromised. This perhaps would be another case of ADHD if he attended regular school, as he was already being considered with ADHD by the Church Sunday School.

These are just two examples of how our children could be misdiagnosed with ADHD when, in reality, all their struggles are linked to their temperament traits and habits. With some understanding and sufficient knowledge about temperament traits, it is possible to change behavior by stopping the nurturing of negative characteristics and focusing on the strength of the child's temperament type.

Some well-known people have also struggled with ADHD and other learning disabilities but succeeded nevertheless. Thomas Alva Edison, the inventor and businessman, found school difficult. As a child, he was considered problematic and hyperactive. He created many inventions in electric power generation, mass communication, sound recording, and motion pictures.

Another personality who was diagnosed with ADHD at the age of 9 is Michael Phelps, the 12-time Olympic medal winner swimmer—the most of any athlete in history to this day. If he didn't want to read as a child, his mom would let him read the newspaper's sports section, recognizing and utilizing his interest in sports to improve his reading skills. His mom supported him and encouraged him to swim. When he started swimming, he said he saw an improvement in his concentration and developed self-discipline.

If your child is struggling and everyone, including their school teachers, is telling you that your child has ADHD, before you jump to conclusions, try to identify and understand your child's temperament trait. It may open up an entirely different explanation for your child's struggles, as it did with our daughter. With enough patience and understanding, it is possible to push back on the negative traits and nurture the positives of your child's temperament to improve their behavior and performance.

If, even after working on supporting your child's strong suits and not nurturing their negative traits, things don't change, then do consult a psychologist. Your child might actually have ADHD or some other learning disability that needs a professional diagnosis.

Chapter 3: Tailoring Educational Approaches

When our daughter was 4 years old, her sanguine nature made her impatient with activities like coloring; she would rush through it to finish quickly, often showing little attention to detail or, at times, refusing and crying when faced with the task. Understanding that she needed more focused engagement, we decided to sit down with her every night to color together. Recognizing that sanguine individuals often require extra motivation and support to fully engage in tasks, we prioritized this consistent, guided practice. After a couple months, she began to enjoy coloring books, developing a sharp eye for detail, and creating beautiful artwork independently.

For children who have particular temperament types and those with ADHD, it is not easy to learn at the same pace and with the same educational approach in classrooms as other students. They need a little more attention and a different approach. Therefore, as parents and teachers, we should consider these children's needs when planning a class or study material. Some things can be done to help the students.

Strategies For Enhancing Focus and Engagement

Hyperactive children have a lot of energy and like physical activities. Therefore, sitting still for an extended period and listening to lectures is not their cup of tea. They'll get bored and lose focus, affecting their grades and performance. For these children, we can channel their extra energy into hands-on activities that will help them learn and be active at the same time. They can be asked to act out a play, do an art project or a science experiment, or create video or slide presentations on the topic. Younger kids can participate in interactive learning games or educational activities that develop their cognitive skills, such as Lego building or puzzle solving. These activities will challenge them and keep them engaged. The instant feedback will feel rewarding and keep them motivated to keep going. This is called kinesthetic learning, and it helps the students focus their energy and attention.

In school, teachers can take care of certain things and plan the class to include the needs of the children with distraction or too much energy. Hyperactive children often forget to write homework assignments and bring the finished work to school. Teachers can ensure they write down their homework assignments before leaving class and remind them of the submission date the day before. This will lower their chances of forgetting to do and submit their assignments on time. When the actions of hyperactive children disrupt class, teachers can warn them with hand signals or a look and later take them aside to talk and warn them in private. It will help keep the class undisturbed. Make sure to seat the child away from windows and any other distractions and face the teacher so they don't lose focus during the class.

This is no different in a homeschool setting. Parents and teachers should maintain eye contact with the child and write the instructions clearly on the board to keep their attention span. After teaching a topic, if the key points are summarized, it helps the child retain the information better. If there is a class test or quiet study time, ensure the classroom is free of distractions. Rather than having long tests, frequent short quizzes will be more beneficial. Accepting late work and giving a little credit for the partial work they have done will encourage them to do better. Teachers and parents can be more attentive and assist them in these things. Being the parent of a child with these traits or being their teacher is not easy. You'd need a lot of patience, creativity, and consistency to stick with it and not give up. They need us to learn and grow into confident adults.

The Importance of Structure and Routine

Structure and routine are beneficial to any child, but they are even more helpful for children with attention deficits or hyperactivity. Routines mean order and organization, which are difficult to come by otherwise for children with a low attention span. It provides external control and keeps them on track if they derail from the task. It will also help the child build good habits for life because doing it alone is a mountain of a task for them. If routines are set in the home, simply following them with other family members will build healthy habits. Even though routines are essential and helpful, sometimes they also tend to become dull and repetitive. Therefore, it is crucial to add breaks and movement between them. Break tasks into small manageable steps for the child with enough breaks in between. It is tough for them to follow a long string of instructions. Give them one instruction at a time, say it with a pause, and repeat the instructions, which will help them register it. This will help them focus more and feel a sense of accomplishment after every small task leading up to the bigger task. During these breaks, getting enough movement will release excess energy, improve focus and cognitive function, and help them retain information better. When creating structure and routines for the child, the space for flexibility should also be given. The structure should be developed, changed, and altered per the child's changing needs.

Children with these characteristics can perform better when they have a visual display of their schedules and study materials. They are visual learners and need visual aids like charts, pictures, or color codes. Use visual planners to help the child understand and follow the daily and weekly routines. Print it out and stick it to the wall or somewhere they can always see it. They will not forget or get distracted so quickly when it is in front of them. In the same way, the study materials can also be printed out and stuck to their table or in the room so that they can learn better. When it is displayed right in front of them, it becomes highly unlikely that they will ignore it or get distracted.

Innovative Teaching Methods for Diverse Learners

Children who struggle with hyperactivity, impulsivity, and inattention have a challenging learning journey. A one-size-fits-all curriculum and teaching approach will not benefit these children. That is why we need differentiated instruction in classrooms. Regardless of their backgrounds, abilities, temperament traits, and interests, differentiated instruction is important to all students as it supports their individual strengths and promotes student engagement. Differentiated instruction involves creating an accommodating classroom environment and tailoring the instructions to accommodate the student's special needs, which will promote their academic success. For effective differentiation in the classroom, the following tips can be used.

Predictable and Well-Structured Environment

In a predictable and well-structured environment, children experience less anxiety and confusion, helping them focus and thrive. Establishing rules and routines for the students can help. Maintaining a regular schedule will reduce anxiety and uncertainty (Mulligan, 2001). Use visual schedules of the day's tasks and display them in class where everyone can see them.

When giving students instructions and explaining the process of a task, be clear and concise. Split the task into small, manageable mini-tasks and communicate your expectations clearly. Give one or two instructions at a time and repeat them for better understanding. This will ensure that the students aren't overwhelmed by the long instructions.

Include Multi-Sensory Learning

Multi-sensory learning makes learning more interactive, and children have fun while they learn. Engaging multiple senses in the learning process enhances comprehension, concentration, and retention.

To engage their sense of vision, you can use visual aids such as flow charts, diagrams, or mind mapping. Taking down notes can be made more interesting with the use of color coding and highlighters. It will look organized and neat (Remata & Lomibao, 2021).

Auditory elements such as reading out loud, using audio clips, encouraging students to share their ideas in class, and participating in discussions and debates could be used during class. This will promote comprehension and retention.

Tactile learning involves the sense of touch. Building models and creating craft projects using textured and sensory materials helps students be more involved and focus on the task. Kinesthetic learning involves hands-on activities that engage the students physically in a task. Examples include performing plays, doing science experiments, or creating art projects. Movement enhances focus and reduces hyperactivity.

Group Work and Project-Based Learning

Group activities are an excellent way to promote cooperative learning, collaboration, and teamwork. Working in groups means sharing ideas, listening to other's perspectives, and supporting and learning from each other.

The best way to learn is to teach. That is why peer tutoring works well among students. Students can be put into small groups, and every student can be asked to teach a small topic. This will encourage them to prepare well, present them, and learn simultaneously.

Project-based learning involves students working on a complex task for an extended time. It's an efficient and interactive way of learning, which can be very engaging for students. It encourages students to self-drive their learning and develop critical thinking, problem-solving, and self-management skills.

Using Technology for Differentiated Learning

Interactive technology can be used to make classroom learning more exciting and engaging. It will help students from feeling bored and losing focus. Audio tapes, podcasts, and audiobooks can be used as teaching aids. Complex concepts can be better explained through presentations and videos. Using modern technology in moderation can be an excellent way to make the class engaging for neurodivergent students.

Emotional and Behavioral Support

Students should be provided with emotional and behavioral support in addition to academics. Create a safe space and build good relationships with the students so they open up about their struggles and emotions. Please encourage them to share their thoughts and teach them self-regulation techniques.

Success Without Medication: Alternatives in Education

Medication should always be the last resort. Before resorting to medication, we, as parents and teachers, should do our best to try out every way we can help our children with challenging temperament traits. Addressing their emotional needs will reduce behavioral problems, boost confidence, and create a positive learning environment. Here are some ways to help students who need extra care in the learning environment.

Emotional and Behavioral Support/ Strategies

The overall development of the child should be the main focus. Focusing only on academics will not help the child and complicate things further. Understanding and supporting their emotional and behavioral needs is as crucial as their academics. This can be done in various ways. Firstly, creating a positive growth-oriented mindset is essential to every student's emotional well-being. Create a supportive environment where students can express their emotions without judgment. This can be providing opportunities for one-on-one conversation or group discussions. Also, teaching them emotional vocabulary and social-emotional learning (SEL) skills will help them express their emotions better and understand others. In addition to expressing their feelings well, it is also vital to learn self-regulation strategies such as deep breathing, mindfulness, and visualization to manage one's behavior, emotions, and thoughts for improved social interactions. Self-regulation is only possible when they can understand their strengths and weaknesses, know their rights, and communicate them efficiently. For this, we can teach them to express their needs appropriately and ask for help when needed through activities like role-playing scenarios. Children should be made aware of when their behaviors are inappropriate and that there are consequences, like losing certain privileges. Involve them to discuss why their behavior was unacceptable and help them explore better alternatives.

Environmental Modifications

The environment kids are in can impact the quality of their learning and productivity. Therefore, when designing or setting up a classroom, if certain things are considered, it can significantly help the children focus and pay attention during classes. Educators can create the optimal learning environment for every child by designing the classrooms and structuring the class layout while considering the following things.

Overall Layout and Seating Arrangements

When it comes to seating arrangements, using traditional row seating is the best. The child with ADHD and temperaments prone to distractions should be seated close to the teacher to reduce getting distracted during class. Children with ADHD need their quiet time. It helps them cope better. Therefore, providing a silent corner table for children to use during quiet study time or when they need some alone time will help them.

Visual Aids

Like we stated before, displaying the classroom schedule and the due dates for the assignments on a chart in the classroom where everyone can see them will ensure that every child remembers them. Knowing the daily schedule beforehand helps children feel organized and mentally prepare better for the upcoming class. Using real-life models, flow charts, and experiments to explain concepts will help the children better grasp and remember what has been taught in class.

Manage Classroom Humidity

Humidity also plays an important part in keeping the environment comfortable and optimal for learning. An increase or a decrease in the classroom's humidity will make the students uncomfortable, leading to potential distractions. Increasing humidity will make the space feel oppressive, and low humidity can cause dry eyes and skin irritation. Automation-triggered sensors will trigger actions like adjusting HVAC systems or activating dehumidifiers to monitor classroom humidity and keep it conducive to learning.

Colors of the Classroom

Selecting the right colors for the classroom is essential to keeping the classroom free of sensory stimuli. Bold colors like neon or red should be avoided. Using bold colors in the study environment will elevate blood pressure and cause anxiety, depression, or even anger in some children. To minimize the stimuli, soft, soothing, neutral, and warm colors should be used in classrooms.

Interior Lighting

Interior lighting is as important as selecting the right colors. Some kids have photophobia and a great sensitivity to bright lights. When designing the learning space, focus on reflections, glare, and shadow patterns to create a non-distracting environment. Soothing lights should be used for optimal environmental conditions for better learning.

Acoustics

The acoustics of the building depend on the way a space is designed, its form, and its finishes. A building or classroom with good acoustics helps with speech, attention, hypersensitivity, and auditory processing issues. In a classroom setting, both noises from outside and other background noises should be kept out. Good acoustics make sure that the background noises and reverberations are limited. It can be done by using sealed insulation windows and building the walls, ceiling, and floors using sound-absorbing materials and those with high NPC ratings.

Importance of Recreation and Physical Activity

It has been found that spending time in nature can be soothing to both children and adults alike by reducing stress and anxiety. Also, the attention span gets a healthy boost (Robbins, 2020). Temperament traits and ADHD symptoms can be better managed if children play outside in parks, playgrounds, and sensory gardens instead of sitting all day inside a classroom. They provide a secure environment for kids to develop their senses without being overwhelmed. Having dedicated time each day when children can be outside exploring and playing will help them lose a lot of excess energy and focus and learn better during class.

Natural Remedies and Dietary Considerations

Case studies have found that a proper diet and some natural remedies are beneficial in reducing ADHD symptoms and will support the child's educational strategies and overall well-being (Pinto et al., 2022).

Diet and Nutrition

Eating well contributes to any child's positive development and performance, not just children with ADHD. But in the case of children with ADHD, getting proper nutrition from eating the right food and avoiding certain foods has been seen to bring an immense change to their performance and symptoms.

One crucial factor is regularly monitoring your child's blood sugar levels. A spike in their glycemic index means the body will try to drop that sugar level, bringing it to below-normal levels and causing the child to be irritable, fidgety, and nervous. Ensure that your child's meals, especially breakfast, are free of high sugar levels.

Avoid refined, processed, and sugar-loaded foods as much as possible. Frozen waffles, Pop-Tarts, cookies, white bread, cakes, and similar products will shoot the blood sugar levels to alarming rates. Also, avoiding pesticide-laden vegetables, processed meat, food colorings, and preservatives is highly recommended. Some studies say that pesticides in our food may also contribute to the development of ADHD (Bouchard et al., 2010). Specific colors and preservatives have increased hyperactive behavior in children (Arnold et al., 2012). Therefore, opting for whole, organic foods is recommended.

For a balanced diet, including organic vegetables and fruits; complex carbohydrates like brown rice, beans, and lentils; sources of protein such as beans, soy, nuts, eggs, and plant-based milk; healthy fats like tofu, avocado, and coconut oil, sources of vitamins and minerals like leafy greens, fruits and veggies.

Natural Supplements

Talk to your child's pediatrician and give them the required supplements. Giving flaxseed oil supplements to children with ADHD will make up for their lack of omega-3s, which will provide a boost to their brain functioning. Iron, vitamin D, and zinc deficiency are also common in children with ADHD. Iron deficiency causes irregular dopamine production in the brain, and deficiency of vitamin D and zinc elevates other ADHD symptoms. Taking supplements for these deficiencies will help reduce ADHD symptoms. Though magnesium levels tend to be normal in most children, magnesium supplements may have a calming effect on kids who have trouble sleeping.

Sleep

Children with ADHD and particular temperament traits already suffer from a variety of sleep dysfunctions, like difficulty falling asleep. Therefore, quality sleep is essential to their overall functioning. Ensure your child goes to bed and wakes up around the same time daily. Help them create a nighttime routine like reading a book, taking a cold shower before bedtime, and dimming all the lights in the house for a good quality sleep. A good night's sleep helps with managing symptoms.

Screen Time

Excessive screen time in children causes issues like emotional dysregulation, poor mental health, poor quality sleep, poor academic performance, and even developmental delays. It increases the symptoms of ADHD in children. Getting rid of screen time altogether may not be possible in this era, but as parents, we can regulate the time our children spend in front of screens. Create screen time rules to follow at home and control the time spent in front of the television or through social media. This will have a massive impact on the mental health of our kids.

Stress Management

Most children with ADHD characteristics are very sensitive to stress. You can use some strategies to help your child deal with stress. Help your child with the things they are good at. It will boost their self-esteem. Build a good family relationship and a soothing home environment so that they have you to come whenever something bothers them. Monitor their feedback from school and help them overcome their weaknesses. Hear them patiently and show compassion when they come to you for help. Knowing that their parents are there for them will help mitigate the stress.

Daily Devotional or Meditation

Meditating or participating in a daily devotional can help calm the brain, thus reducing the intensity of ADHD symptoms. It can also help improve hyperactivity, anxiety, and social problems, regulate distractions, and enhance focus.

Outdoor Time and Exercise

Good physical activity and time outside in nature boosts the dopamine in one's brain. It also helps with improved concentration and reduces hyperactivity.

Medication should be the last resort when it comes to taking care of our children. Even if there is a need for medication, doing these natural remedies and following a healthy ADHD-friendly dietary plan in addition to that will go a long way in helping your child live an easier life.

Create a Home Environment Conducive to Learning

Because of hyperactivity and a lack of continued focus, children with ADHD and temperament differences often do not perform well academically. It is not that they don't have the ability; they can excel if they can focus on one task at a time and not get distracted by their space and thoughts. Creating a structure and using methods to minimize distractions will help them learn better. Some ways to do this are as follows.

Homework Routines

When children follow routines religiously and consistently each day, they become more disciplined. Homework routines help children stay organized, helping them know what to expect and mentally prepare for it. They also make them productive and focused. Following routines will instill a sense of order in your child, which will mold their character and help them later in life, in college, and at work.

Making your hyperactive and attention-deficit child sit still to complete their homework on time every day is not easy, but it is possible. There are some things parents can do to keep them motivated to follow a daily homework routine.

The three key questions to set a successful homework routine are: When? Where? And how?

When

Set a time after school to do homework each day. If your child is hyperactive and needs to release some energy before sitting down to study, let them play or do something they like for an hour before starting the homework routine. However, it is best not to push homework time to late evenings because they will likely be tired by then, and some children may have a meltdown. Depending on their history of completing homework and their grade level, schedule enough time to complete all the assignments with enough breaks in between to keep them motivated. The breaks can be after completing an assignment or after some time as per their need. Set a timer to indicate the start and the completion of the time allocated for homework. When their homework time is about to start, inform them beforehand that they soon need to stop doing whatever they are doing and start working on their homework. If not reminded, children tend to get so involved in their exciting activities that they forget about boring stuff like homework.

Where

Create a dedicated study space for your child. Sitting down to do their homework with their siblings or in a common area may not work well for your child with ADHD or temperament differences. It will be too distracting. Create dedicated study spaces for your child to sit down and study. Make the space devoid of anything like toys, electronics, and other things unrelated to studying. If possible, face the table away from the window and in a silent area of the house. A table and chair with only a clock and their study materials will do. Ensure the child uses that space only for studies, not for anything like eating, playing video games, or watching movies. It has to be a dedicated study space so that when the child is there, their mind knows it's time to study and not wander off to do anything else. Dedicated study spaces help maintain your child's focus on studying and getting their homework done.

How

Print out the homework schedule specifying the start and end times, when the breaks will happen, for how long, and what they can do during breaks. Display it in their study space or somewhere your child can see it. Be available and let them know you are there if they need help understanding the assignments, but don't do the homework for them. Help them start by ensuring they understand the assignment and how to start. If they are a verbal learner, reading the assignment directions or having them read them aloud will help them understand better. If your child is a visual learner, showing them how to use study tools like Post-It notes and highlighters effectively will make studying easier for them. Your child may want to give up before completing the assignment or take more frequent breaks than scheduled. In that case, encourage them to keep going with your words, let them know that the next break will be there soon, or promise a small reward like extra playtime if they are struggling. If it becomes too overwhelming for your child, let them take a break and return later to complete the assignment. Offering praise and the promise of a reward at the end is a strong motivator for the child to stick with it and complete their homework on time. Simple incentives for completing their homework, like extra playtime, or their favorite healthy treat, give them something to look forward to. After they are done, review their work and ensure they have completed all the assignments.

The most essential part of any schedule is consistency. Do the same thing daily to make it a routine, and in time, it will become a habit. For children with ADHD and temperament differences, it is harder to stick to routines and maintain their focus; they'll get bored quickly. However, the right amount of praise, small rewards, and your presence can help them develop a better study habit, improving their academic performance.

Balancing Academics and Leisure

Academics is one of the most important parts of a child's life. But that is not all that is to their life. Children need a healthy balance of learning and playtime to grow into physically, mentally, and intellectually healthy individuals. Give your child the time and space to be creative, play with their friends outside, with their siblings, or do their favorite activities. Make sure that they are physically active. Physical activity is crucial for brain development. You can join them in their leisure time. Play with them, create art or crafts projects, and help them with their creative innovations. Children learn better through play. When it is time to study, be with them to keep them focused and help them in need. Let them enjoy their free time as they like. A healthy blend of academics and leisure raises a child into a confident and healthy adult.

Make a Difference with Your Review: Unlock the Power of Generosity

"True joy comes from giving to others, not from receiving." - Unknown

People who give selflessly often find greater happiness in their lives. Let's spread that joy together!

Most people decide which books to read based on reviews. By sharing your thoughts, you can assist fellow parents and readers in discovering this helpful guide.

It costs nothing and takes less than a minute but could make a big difference in someone's journey.

To make a difference, simply scan the QR code below and leave a review.

Thank you for your support!

Ghee & Bee

Chapter 4: Positive Behavior Support Systems

We'll never forget the summer of 2016 when our family visited for a few weeks. At the time, one of our nephews was just a year old, only six months younger than our daughter, and struggled to communicate, often resorting to screaming for attention and crying out of frustration. He appeared to be developing more slowly compared to his older brother and displayed signs of attention deficit and hyperactivity. However, his sanguine temperament, humid over hot—evidenced by his loving, sweet demeanor and eagerness to help others—became apparent as he grew older. We noticed similar traits in our own daughter, who also has a sanguine breeze temperament. Early on, we taught her how to communicate through simple signs, which made a significant difference. This early experience underscored the importance of understanding and accommodating different temperaments. It taught us the value of patience and customized support in nurturing a child's emotional growth, revealing how our nephew's and daughter's inherent qualities would blossom with the right encouragement.

Understanding the Behavior in Each Temperament

Children don't display their best behavior at all times. But if they are constantly showcasing negative behaviors, then there might be a hidden reason that needs to be identified and solved for the healthy development of your child.

Behavior as Communication

Our behaviors are a response to our environments and situations. It is a form of expression. In the same way, children's behavior from a very young age is a form of expressing themselves. There is always a reason behind their engaging in negative behavior. It is their way of communicating with us. Seeing a child's negative behavior as a form of communication forces us to consider why they are showing disruptive behavior. Labeling children as "good" if they are very obedient and as "bad" if they don't conform to the norms is not the right way to deal with negative behaviors. Doing so will make the children who show negative behavior feel like they are as they are and cannot change. When children get overwhelmed by strong feelings and cannot put them into words, they may cry, shout, or show others negative behaviors. Parents and teachers should change their perspective and try to understand what the child may be going through. Scolding or spanking them is not the way to go.

Identifying Triggers

The first step in understanding what is happening with the child is identifying the triggers for such behaviors. Start by looking at how the situation or environment has changed before and after the child's behavior. Were there any recent changes in their routines, their friend circle, the time of the day it usually happens, or any other social situation at home or school that might be acting as a trigger for your child? Identifying and understanding their temperament trait will give a better perspective on their behaviors. You will be able to know if the behavior is a characteristic of their temperament type and how you can help them. By focusing on your child's communication rather than labeling them as "bad" or "good," you can focus on the triggers and finding strategies to help them.

Some factors that affect children's behavior are temperament, development stages, disability, and a change in environment or routines.

The four temperament types—sanguine, choleric, melancholic, and phlegmatic—have different qualities, and children with each temperament have different ways of dealing with new situations and emotions and different responses to them.

Children with phlegmatic temperaments are easygoing and usually adapt well to new environments and people. Their parents may not have much trouble with their behavior.

Children with sanguine temperaments may be cheerful most of the time, but as they are people-pleasers, they might struggle a lot. This may come out in the form of tantrums or meltdowns.

The melancholic children who prefer solitude don't seem to have much trouble, but like children with sanguine temperaments, they too have some though times when putting their emotions into words becomes difficult.

Children with choleric temperaments are known as troublemakers. They are hot-headed and dominating and often end up making trouble. A look into your child's temperament will give a good perspective into the reason behind their behavior. The way they deal with a situation depends on their temperament.

Children go through developmental stages as they grow. From the infant stage to becoming an adult, various developmental milestones exist, such as crawling, talking, height, and weight. These milestones are the level of physical, mental, emotional, and reasoning skills that the child must achieve at every stage of their life—knowing what developmental milestone to reach what age helps parents monitor their children's growth. Developmental delays will affect the child's ability to communicate appropriately. That might be the reason for their negative behavior. So, as parents, we should keep track of our children's growth and development.

It is also possible that an undiagnosed disability might be the trigger for your child's negative behavior. Children with ADHD might find it difficult to stay put in a social situation, a child with sensory disorder will find noisy, crowded spaces uncomfortable, or a child with autism may not be able to interact comfortably with other children. Such children are not able to communicate their feelings and emotions properly and throw tantrums. That is their way of saying that they are struggling and need help.

The Impact of the Environment

The environment a child grows up in and does their learning in significantly impacts their development and behavior. Constantly exposing children to loud noises and chaos, like high-volume television or fighting parents, is found to affect their cognitive development and cause psychological distress. Their long-term memory and reading abilities are affected. They reach these milestones slower than other children their age and often struggle later. Children growing up in troubled homes develop an unhealthy understanding of relationships, and they will find it challenging to integrate appropriately into social situations. For children with ADHD, too much exposure to bright light and colors can be triggering. Some children find socializing hard and feel frustrated in social gatherings and classrooms.

When the environment they are in starts to affect their emotions and mental health, making them overwhelmed, children try to find ways to deal with it, and it comes out through their behavior. Some kids isolate themselves and retreat from situations they are not comfortable with. Others may throw tantrums when things don't go their way. Knowing the root cause of this behavior will help in dealing with the child's negative behavior the right way. Observe their environments at home and school, know their friends and who they hang out with in school in the neighborhood, talk to them, and make the necessary changes to encourage and support proper behavior in your child.

Positive Reinforcement: Rewarding Desired Behaviors

One way of eliminating negative behavior and encouraging positive behavior in children is through positive reinforcement. Children with ADHD find the reward system appealing, encouraging them to work harder and improve.

Principles of Positive Reinforcement

The principle of positive reinforcement encourages children to behave well by focusing on their positive behaviors and rewarding them. It is one of the most effective behavior modification techniques. We understand that when your child misbehaves, you might be more inclined to punish them than to think about rewards. However, this method has proven to be effective behavior therapy.

Thorndike's "Law of Effect" theory states that a behavior followed by pleasant or desirable consequences will likely be repeated. In contrast, behavior that is followed by undesirable consequences is less likely to be repeated (McLeod, 2024). From Thorndike's theory, behaviorist B.F Skinner developed his operant conditioning model based on the assumption that identifying and evaluating a behavior's cause and its consequences is the ideal way to understand and regulate it. This model outlines four methods of conditioning: positive reinforcement, positive punishment, negative reinforcement, and negative punishment. These conditioning methods can be implemented to teach, train, and regulate behavior in children. However, that doesn't mean they are all good. Studies have shown that positive reinforcement is the best way to regulate behavior in children.

Positive reinforcement introduces a pleasant and desirable stimulus after a good behavior. This will reinforce the behavior and increase the chances of repetition of the same behavior. It focuses on the good behavior that the child already displays, rewarding the natural tendencies towards their good behavior.

Implementing Reward Systems

When children feel validated for their good behavior, it will likely be repeated and eventually become habitual. Even in adults, this strategy works. The paycheck at the end of the month is a positive reward for working at our job. The anticipation of the money we earn and the social status that comes with it pushes us to go on even when it gets rough. The same is the case with children.

Encouragement, kindness, consistency, and limit setting are the four pillars of positive reinforcement. Various non-expensive and uncomplicated ways to positively reinforce a child's behavior exist. It can be done through pleasant gestures like hugging, clapping, high-fiving, or giving them a pat on the back. Words of encouragement are also effective. You can praise them in front of everyone, tell them you are proud of them, and support their behavior. Another way is rewarding them with an activity, giving them extra privileges, or anything else they desire. It can allow them to play a little longer, watch that kids' show for twenty minutes, or go to the park together. Token systems where you can exchange your tokens for a bigger reward also instill consistent positive behavior. Giving your child the option to choose their reward for consistent good behavior will motivate them and build a sense of agency.

Immediate vs. Delayed Rewards

As adults, we can keep calm and wait for our paycheck at the end of each month for our hard work. However, children are not that patient. With children, an immediate reward for their positive behavior is more effective. They'll likely misbehave if you make them wait a month to reward their efforts. Please don't wait for the right moment; let them know they are doing great. Praise your children's efforts, and show your love and support. It affects their mental health, growth, and behavior more than you know. Children grow up to be responsible adults and integrate well within society when they get recognition and unconditional love from their parents at a young age. Immediate rewards encourage children, especially kids with ADHD, to continue with their good behavior, eventually molding their personality.

Avoiding Over-Reliance on Material Rewards

When we say rewards, we immediately think of material gifts. But that is not necessarily the case. Material rewards in moderation are good. However, gifting your children the latest toys, gadgets, clothes, and other stuff will not be beneficial in the long run. It will only make them over-reliant on materialistic things. Getting them something they want as a positive reinforcement for consistently showcasing a certain behavior is good, but only some rewards should be materialistic. Parents and teachers can adopt positive reinforcement methods to build character and reinforce good behavior in children. You can transform your child's behavior and help them improve daily.

Managing Meltdowns With Empathy and Strategy

Understanding Meltdowns

Children, especially toddlers, have emotional rollercoaster rides all day long. In a single day, you can see them go from happy to frustrated to sad to giggling again. Young children cannot control and regulate their emotions. When frustrated and dissatisfied, they misbehave and throw tantrums. Managing child tantrums and meltdowns is one of the biggest challenges of parenting. If not dealt with carefully, it can manifest into more significant problems as children grow up. Tantrums and meltdowns may sound the same, but they are very different. Tantrums are milder outbursts with the child still having some control over their behavior. Tantrums subside when they realize their behavior will not get them the desired outcome. During a meltdown, a child completely loses control over their body, and the behavior stops when the parent can calm them down, or they wear themselves out.

A child throws a tantrum or goes into a complete meltdown when they feel like something they desire is being deliberately held back from them, and they feel unfairly treated. A meltdown is the result of severe distress and anxiety. They are not able to regulate their emotions and get angry and start crying uncontrollably. If you notice that these meltdowns happen regularly, there might be some other underlying causes, like delay in developing emotional regulation, which can be a result of an underlying problem like ADHD, anxiety, learning problems, depression, or autism. Consider consulting a child psychologist or counselor if your child has frequent meltdowns.

Prevention Strategies

Total prevention may not be possible, but there are some strategies we can use to try to stop tantrums before they start or prevent tantrums from developing into meltdowns. We can observe our children to identify the triggers that cause the onset of these behaviors. There is always a reason for the child's tantrum and meltdown. It can be as simple as separation anxiety when you get them out of the house to drop them at daycare or a feeling of injustice when their piece of cake is slightly smaller than their brother's. Good observation will tell you what your child is going through emotionally during the meltdown and give insight into what your child needs.

Some strategies to try and prevent the onset of tantrums and meltdowns are:

- Discuss what frustration feels like and what to do when they feel frustrated. Openly talk about this emotion and let them know they can come to tell you or signal when they feel frustrated. This way, you can resolve the issue before it manifests into a meltdown or even a tantrum.

- Setting clear expectations about how you expect them to behave gives a clear message. What we agreed and the consequences if it's not followed. We call deals and consequences. They need to know they cannot set the rules.

- Positive reinforcement is another way to promote good behavior. With positive reinforcement, children are less likely to act out when frustrated. They will know how to handle their emotions better over time.

- In some cases, they might be making a scene for your attention. Be firm, showing your authority thru your voice, eye contact and body language. Talk to them once they calm down and understand why they are hurt or struggling.

Be calm, patient, and firm when you see signs of a potential outburst. Engage with your child, and never shout above them, as it will only escalate the situation. Your patience is your best friend here. When you talk to them firmly and calmly, they eventually calm down, possibly preventing the meltdown.

Post-Meltdown Conversations

After a meltdown, your child will be emotionally and physically exhausted. Give them a glass of water and space to calm down. When they are calm, sit with them and let them talk. They might feel embarrassed, but assure them you are there to help them.

Not right after a meltdown, but later, you can help your child learn some coping strategies to deal with their emotions. Let them know that they are allowed to feel sad and frustrated. Still, the way they express their feelings should be regulated and acceptable. They cannot just start screaming or throwing things. Discuss with them how they can try to calm their emotions using methods like deep breaths, praying, sing a song, or talking to you about their feelings.

Parenting is hard, and managing your child's emotional outbursts is the hardest part. However, with proper care, patience, and proper conversations, we can find ways to help our children deal with their emotions.

Setting up for Success: Structured Routines and Expectations

The Power of Routine

Routines may sometimes feel redundant, but they are the way to a purposeful life. With a proper routine, even adults can keep track of the time and get things done correctly. Routines should be included in our children's lives from a young age. Following routines instills discipline, which is essential for becoming a responsible adult. Having routines at home, like making your bed as soon as you get up, brushing your teeth after meals, and doing your homework every day at the same time, helps the child understand what to expect and be prepared beforehand. For example, they know they can only go out and play if they complete their homework. When things are repeated regularly, it becomes a habit. Good habits build character, and discipline becomes a part of their lives. Examples of some routines that can be followed at home are cleaning their room every weekend, doing their homework before dinner, cleaning their plates after every meal, or assigning 30 minutes every evening as family time to talk and bond.

When creating routines, some things can be considered for maximum benefit.

Clear Expectations

Every routine should have a goal. Your expectations of your child should be made clear by following that routine. They should know what they are expected to do and how to behave. Children should be made a part of the decision-making process. When creating a routine for their chores or studies, include them in the discussion. Before making a decision, take into account their suggestions too. It will make them feel included in the creation process and more enthusiastic about following the routines as they have a say in making them.

Use visual aids to better let them know your expectations, such as displaying the routines in a printout format on the fridge or anywhere your children can see them. Create a small progress chart or calendar to tick off the days the schedule or chores were followed. It will act as an encouragement.

In schools and classrooms, displaying the schedule for the day and due dates of assignments and projects where the students see them gives them an idea of what to expect.

Routines and schedules make kids less anxious about the future and what is expected of them. Knowing what is coming next and how they are supposed to behave gives them confidence as they are mentally prepared for it. Children with ADHD and difficult temperaments find it especially useful to know the schedule to regulate their emotions and not get overwhelmed in difficult situations.

Flexibility Within Structure

As adults, we sometimes become too strict with our children about following the rules and routines, leading to conflicts. As adults, we sometimes find it challenging to stick to our routines, so how can we expect our children to always be perfect? Rules and routines are there for the well-being of our children; if they are causing distress, it is a sign that something needs to be changed. The routines should be flexible at times. Not all days are the same. Sometimes, our kids might have had a bad day at school and need some consolation or time alone. At such a time, pestering them about finishing their chores is not a good idea. They also need the space to regulate their emotions. So, as parents, we must teach routines in our children's lives to make them disciplined. However, it should not come at the price of their mental health. Make the routines per your child's needs and capacity and change them to suit their needs as and when required. To avoid redundancy, you can make changes occasionally so your child sticks to the routines.

Sleep Strategies

Sleep is essential to the proper functioning of the human body. On average, adults need eight hours of sleep every night. A lack of sleep over a long period will increase the chances of Alzheimer's and other neurological diseases. Getting enough sleep is crucial to young children's growth and development. Children need more sleep than adults because they are still growing and developing. Not getting enough sleep will make kids fussy and restless. They will have mood swings and show impulsive behavior. It can affect their memory and focus. They might develop learning problems and eating disorders. Sleeping well and for the required number of hours is essential to children's good health.

You can look for some of the signs of a sleeping disorder. If your child cannot sleep well occasionally, it should not be a problem. But if you think they are not sleeping well almost every day, then you might have a problem. You can observe and look for some of the signs of this disorder. Some of these symptoms are bedwetting, sleepy and yawning during the daytime, falling asleep in class or during the day at home, not wanting to wake up in the morning, snoring, restless sleep, decreased performance, and less active during the day and trouble falling asleep at night. Your child may have one of these signs or a combination of a few. If you see these signs in them, you need to find the underlying cause of it.

Sometimes, as much as we might want to get a good night's sleep, it becomes an impossible task to achieve. Children develop sleep issues for several reasons. Some causes of these issues in children may be their daytime behavior and inconsistent bedtimes. If children over-exhaust themselves during the day or take too many or too long of naps, it can affect their sleep at night. These causes can easily be remedied, and your child's sleep troubles can be resolved at home with some effort. The causes like obesity and restless leg syndrome, on the other hand, will require professional advice.

Recommended sleep hours for children as per their age are:

Birth to 1 year (infants): 12 to 16 hours

1 to 2 years (toddlers): 11 to 14 hours

3 to 5 years (children): 10 to 13 hours

6 to 12 years (children): 9 to 12 hours

13 to 18 years (teenagers): 8 to 12 hours

If your child is not sleeping within these ranges for their age group, they might have a sleep problem. Some commonly seen sleep disorders are insomnia, sleep apnea, sleepwalking, and nightmares.

Establishing a Sleep Routine and Sleep Environment

The first and the best way to deal with a sleep disorder is to follow a sleep routine every night. You can also call it the night routine because it includes certain things to be done before you hit the bed. Encouraging your child to follow a night routine and doing it with them will help regulate their sleep schedule.

It is imperative that the child goes to bed and wakes up at the same time every single day, including weekends. For the best result, make them go to bed early and wake them up early. Our bodies have a 24-hour natural clock that tells us when to sleep and wake up. This internal clock is in sync with environmental cues like light and darkness, regulating our bodies' alertness and sleepiness cycles.

Creating soothing rituals to follow daily before sleep time, like reading before bed or a cold shower, calms and relaxes the body, essential to a good night's sleep. Ensure the child has no heavy meals right before bed, and all devices should be put away at least one hour before bedtime. Also, getting rid of or limiting daytime naps will help your child sleep better at night. When it comes to the bedroom, make it a place where the child only sleeps and not where he plays or does his homework. In doing so, when they enter the bedroom, their mind will automatically know that it's a sleeping space and they need to sleep now. Keep the bed plain and clear of any distractions like toys or books. Dim all the lights close to bedtime, switch off the television, and keep aside all personal devices. The bedroom should be silent, cold, and dark. It induces sleep. When it is time to wake your child in the morning, open the blinds and let the sunshine bathe them. Sunshine will wake them up energized and ready for the day.

This is not possible overnight, but religiously following the routine every night makes it easier to get in the rhythm. After some time, your child will start feeling sleepy at bedtime and will wake up even without an alarm clock.

When to Seek Help

When things don't get better even after trying sleep rituals and maintaining the sleep-inducing environment, your child's sleep problem might have another underlying cause. If your child still has sleep disturbances, chronic sleep loss, and unusual symptoms that are affecting their daily life, then it is recommended to consult a professional. Talk to your child's pediatrician to seek professional help.

The Impact of Screen Time: Guidelines for Parents

The WHO recommends that children below two years old should have zero screen time, and those between two and four years old should only have a maximum of 1 hour a day (WHO, 2019). We know that it is easier to give them a tablet so that you can get your work or chores done. Sometimes, you are so exhausted that you don't have the energy to play with them or deal with their tantrums. It feels easier to give up and let them watch some kid's show for some time. But this comes with a heavy price. Excessive screen time will negatively affect their growth. Young children are supposed to run around and play and not sit in front of a screen for hours. They need to be active for healthy growth.

Effects of Screen Time on Children

Excessive screen time is harmful to children. Kids get overstimulated, and that will affect their productivity and day-to-day functioning drastically.

When babies constantly watch television or videos on phones or tablets, their developmental milestones are delayed. Some children develop speech delays because they interact with the screen more than with the people around them. Babies need only their parents, and screens are the worst thing to hand them. Spending too much time looking at screens will also affect their cognitive and socio-emotional growth. It will lead to a short attention span, low empathy, mental health disorders, sleep disorders, and even obesity in children because of too little active time. When children spend a large amount of their daily time on social media and watching videos, the time they spend interacting with their parents and siblings is substantially reduced, and they often need more quality family time. It will weaken the parent-child bond, and their ability to interpret emotions gets obstructed, leading to aggressive conduct and harming their psychological health.

A cohort study was conducted between July 2013 and March 2017 under the Tohoku Medical Megabank Project Birth and Three Generation Cohort Study to examine the association between screen time exposure among one-year-old children and the five domains of developmental delay—communication, fine motor, gross motor, problem-solving, and social and personal skills (Kuriyama et al., 2019). Seven thousand ninety-seven mother-child pairs were analyzed for this study. It revealed that for children aged one year, too much screen time was associated with developmental delays in problem-solving and communication at ages two and four.

Eliminating screen time altogether from older kids' lives is not possible or even practical. Therefore, we need to find a balance and set limits for daily screen time.

Setting Limits

The amount of time our children spend in front of the television and other screens can only be limited if the parents intervene and set the rules. The screen time for teens can only be reduced by including specific elements or activities specifically aimed at reducing it. When parents restrict the use of technology like television, mobile phones, tablets, computers, or video games, children end up spending less time on screens. One way to restrict screen time is by using parental controls that come with almost every device. You can activate it in the extra settings. This way, the child will lose access after the time is up, and you can also control the shows that your child watches.

Create technology-free zones in your home where screens, be it phones, tablets, or video games, are not allowed, no matter what. For example, the dining table should be a space for the family to come together for a meal and conversation. Keep the devices away when you are having quality time. Don't watch television or be on your phone in front of your child when he is studying. It will distract them and affect their focus.

Eliminating screen time is challenging with older children, and therefore, it is essential to focus on the quality and quantity of this activity. We can make the time our children spend in front of screens beneficial. Make your children watch age-appropriate educational shows with you, which can be a positive learning experience. By watching educational content together, you can connect with and have an interactive experience with your child. Avoid mainstream and commercial programs and short videos that will affect your child's attention span.

Another way to limit screen time is to involve your child in activities they will enjoy and keep them busy. When you need time to get things done, you can give them a puzzle, coloring materials, a book to read, or toys to play with. If you are concerned for your child's safety, you can always use a playpen or a high chair to ensure they don't end up falling or climbing over things. Instead of giving them your phone or tablet to play games or watch videos, engaging them in activities like reading or drawing will drastically reduce their screen time and the possibility of dependence on them in the future. Take them to parks, encourage them to play with their friends outside, and spend time with them doing activities they love.

Young children need to learn the difference between chores and play. Toddlers are always interested in doing what they see their parents doing. So, the next time they want to do the laundry with you, let them help you load the washing machine. This will teach good habits, help them develop valuable skills, and keep them away from screens.

Parents must follow their own advice by restricting their children's screen time. Don't keep swiping through reels all day or leave the television on when they come home from school. Children imitate what they see.

Techniques for Reducing Stress and Anxiety

Stress is a natural reaction when faced with a challenging or threatening situation. In comparison, anxiety is a persistent feeling of dread that doesn't go away even when the concern has passed. Everyone experiences stress in challenging circumstances, but long-term stress can harm our physical and mental health. Chronic stress causes high blood pressure, heart disease, obesity, a weakened immune system, anxiety, and depression.

In both elementary and secondary education, an increasing number of children are suffering from anxiety and other stress-related disorders (Saps et al., 2009).

In a study published in JAMA Pediatrics, annual data from the National Survey of Children's Health of children from birth to 17 years of age were evaluated to examine the recent trends in children's health-related measures. It was observed that from 2016 to 2020, children between the ages of 3 and 17 who were diagnosed with anxiety grew by 29%. Those diagnosed with depression grew by 27% (Lebrun-Harris et al., 2022).

Our children suffer from these conditions that will affect their health and well-being. To help them, we first need to identify the stressors that cause stress among young children.

Identifying Stressors

Children can be under stress at home or school. If the home environment is not peaceful, it becomes a source of stress. Family discord, divorce, parents fighting, or alcoholic parents will stress them out. In schools, they might be struggling because of a bully, a strict teacher, or making new friends. Sometimes, good changes like the arrival of a new sibling, a new house, or a new school can also put young children under stress.

Recognizing when your child is stressed is necessary to identify its source and help them with it. There are some signs you can look out for to know when your child is stressed and struggling. When stressed, children become irritable and angry at the smallest things. They'll be short-tempered and argue with you. You might notice a sudden change in their behavior, and they may start neglecting their responsibilities, like doing homework or taking the dog out for a walk. Some children will encounter trouble sleeping and eating and get sick more often than usual. If you notice these signs in your children, they are probably stressed and need help. If not dealt with in time, stress will turn into anxiety.

The main symptoms of anxiety in young children are worries and fears. In addition to these, other symptoms like excessive tantrums, nausea, shortness of breath, tingling of hands and feet, restlessness or fatigue, loss of focus, disturbed sleep, loss of appetite, and irritability are also indicators of anxiety. Look out for these symptoms to determine if your child is under stress or has anxiety.

Stress Management for Children

The first thing to ensure as a parent is that your child is in a stress-free environment and lives a lifestyle that does not induce stress. Build a healthy routine with a strict bedtime to ensure that they get enough sleep. Children should eat nutritious food all meals. Foods with sugar and caffeine will give a temporary boost, but afterward, it will make the children feel sluggish. In addition to good sleep and nutritious meals, they must move their body regularly. Encourage your child to join a sport or other form of exercise to keep their body moving. A healthy body is the key to a healthy mind. Screen use should be limited, and more time should be given to fun and quiet activities. Get them involved in a hobby to keep them busy without a device. In this digital era, it is difficult to find some quiet away from screens, but it is essential to keep a calm mind. Children, as well as adults, should spend some time outside of their homes and school or office buildings among nature. People who live in an area with lots of trees are less stressed. Trees and fresh air have a positive impact on our thoughts and minds. A walk in the park helps relieve stress. Following a healthy lifestyle and maintaining a quiet environment at home will reduce the chances of stress in your child.

If your child is under stress or anxious, it is essential to maintain your calm and validate their feelings. Get down to your child's eye level and speak clearly and calmly. Let them know that they are safe with you and you will help them get through this. Hold their hands or hug them; it will help calm them down. You can talk about how you have managed your own stress. Sometimes, they might want to talk about their problems and want you to be a good listener. In that case, sit down with them and listen as they talk. Refrain from interrupting and waiting for them to finish before you speak. Parents need to act as guides and not solve all their problems for them. Let them solve the smaller problems themselves so that when things get more challenging, they won't falter and become strong enough to face them.

When your child experiences stress and anxiety, you can help them cope with them by teaching them stress-relief strategies.

Teach your children mindfulness practices. In a study conducted on one hundred and eight adolescents aged 13 to 18 years, it was found that teens who learned mindfulness experienced less mental distress than those who did not (Tan & Martin, 2014). Mindfulness techniques like meditation and breathwork help in reducing many anxiety symptoms. To calm down a stressed-out child, help them do deep breathing exercises by counting to four as they breathe in and then counting to four as they breathe out. Doing this for several minutes will calm down the child.

When your child engages in negative thinking and starts blaming themselves or finding faults in themselves or their situations, help them combat it. When your child uses negative talk like "I am not pretty" or "I am stupid," instead of just disagreeing with them, ask them to think about whether they believe it to be true. Remind them of the times in the past when they thought they were not good enough, but they worked hard and improved. Curbing negative talk is important to keep stress away.

Muscle relaxation exercise is another method to teach your child to help calm a stressed child. You simply lie down and tense and relax each muscle group, starting at the top of your head and working your way down to the tip of your toes. The child needs to tense up each muscle group, then relax it and move on to the next muscle group until the whole body is done.

Sensory activities like playing with sand or water, squeezing stress balls, finger painting, or using play dough to pound and manipulate will help relieve stress. If your child likes music, listening to their favorite songs may help them calm down. Visualizing a favorite place or a happy memory helps to create positive images and thoughts that will help children take their minds off of the upsetting thoughts.

Journaling is a healthy way to keep away stress and also to bring calm when your child is stressed. Maintaining a diary for daily journaling practice will give your child a place to dump all their feelings in and not simultaneously hurt anyone with their words. Expressing our emotions in words helps reduce mental distress and improves overall well-being. Writing about negative feelings will help your child get it all out of their system. In addition to that, writing about their positive feelings and the things they are grateful for daily will make them realize the good in their life, making them feel grateful and happy.

Maintaining a happy environment at home and good communication with your child will go a long way in easing the chances of their developing stress and anxiety. Keep your eyes and ears open to recognize any symptoms that may suggest your child is under stress or has anxiety to hold their hand as they find solutions and get better. If things are not improving, then you should consult a professional and seek help.

Encouraging Independence and Self-Regulation

We want the best for our children and don't want them to struggle. Therefore, whenever we see them struggling to do something, our first instinct is to step in and do it for them. However, doing so will only send a message that they are not capable of handling it on their own, which will impact their self-confidence. Repeatedly helping them out and not letting them find their own way will make your child dependent on you, and they will start to expect help with every little task. This will lead them to grow into dependent adults who lack the confidence to do anything alone.

Advantages of Instilling Independence in Your Child

Encouraging your child to be independent early on in life will only help them in the long run. Teaching them life skills as children will prepare them to handle difficult situations in the future. They learn to take risks, trust their instincts, and become better informed when doing things themselves. It develops the child's self-esteem and improves their frustration tolerance and perseverance. When children try to do things on their own, they will make mistakes and fail before they succeed. It helps them recognize their mistakes and learn to seek help and guidance from adults and friends when they need it. Children will start using their knowledge and skills to solve problems, boosting their confidence and encouraging them to try their hand at other things as well.

Only when kids are challenged do their full potential arise. They develop grit, skills, tenacity, and self-reliance to help them function better when challenged.

Building Independence

You can use the day-to-day experiences of your child at home, in school, or in other social settings to make them self-reliant. Remember when we were kids, we longed to grow up and be like the big kids and grown-ups because they could do anything? Every child feels the same way. They love to be treated like "big kids." Therefore, letting them do "big-kid" tasks with supervision will make them excited to learn and do the tasks by themselves. Young children need to understand the difference between chores and play. Everything is played to them. Hence, letting them help you with the chores, prepare their own snacks, order their own food at a restaurant, or put on their outfit by themselves will make them feel like a big kid who is capable of doing things by themselves. When they do a task, set realistic expectations, give them what they can handle, and allow them to make mistakes. When they struggle, don't jump in right away; let them fight their own battles. Let them know you are there if they need it, but give them space and help just when they ask. Encourage your child to do simple tasks independently by offering them choices with limited options. This way, they will learn to take risks and make decisions, which are essential skills of adult life. Before making them do things independently, show them how they are done and teach them basic self-help skills. It will give the child the confidence to try things on their own.

Another way to encourage your child to be independent and make it easier to achieve is by designing and organizing your home with your child's independence in mind. Put their clothes in the closet at a height accessible to them, place a stool near the sink so that they can clean their plates, and place their shoes at the lowest rack on the shoe stand, simply making the space accessible to them so that they can reach wherever they want to when doing things independently. As a parent, you also need to match their pace. When children try to do things alone, it will take twice as long and be messier. Parents need to give them the space and time to improve every time. Setting a predictable routine and establishing a chore chart at home will give your child a clear picture of what to expect and when to do it. It will make things easier and more predictable.

Consistency is the key to near perfection. Children need to do things independently more often to build life skills. Your child is only learning and is bound to make mistakes and create a mess in your perfectly organized home. To raise them into self-reliant individuals, you must have the utmost patience and empathy towards your child. With encouraging words and some allowances every now and then, your child will gain the confidence and strength to try again and again until they master the skill.

Teaching Self-Regulation

Self-regulation is our ability to understand, manage, and adapt our behavior and reactions to different situations throughout life. It is one of the most crucial life skills to master living in a civilized world. Self-regulation includes regulating your strong emotions like anger or embarrassment, calming down after something exciting or upsetting, and controlling your impulses in these situations. It also means staying focused when working on a task and refocusing your attention on a new task. Self-regulation will help your child behave in a way that will help them get along with others and make friends.

Self-regulation starts early, over the first five years of a child's life. It then develops in toddler and preschool years and grows into adulthood.

Practicing self-regulation will help your child become independent and self-reliant, boosting their confidence. It will help them control impulses and act in socially appropriate ways, which in turn will help them make friends and build good relationships. Self-reliance will equip them well to handle any stress or frustration. They can focus in class, resulting in better academic performance.

Children watch and learn more from their parents and other adults than by listening to a lecture on how to behave. Self-regulation also develops through healthy and responsive relationships between the child and the parent or the caregiver. We can help our children learn self-regulation by teaching them some techniques to deal with difficult situations and modeling self-regulation ourselves.

Establishing a routine helps in learning self-regulation, too. Teach your child how to calm down in case they get upset or too excited through calming-down strategies like listening to music and breathing. Planning ahead for challenging situations also helps when an actual problem arrives. Pretend-play some difficult circumstances and help them navigate and regulate their emotions to learn to negotiate in different conditions. When they face deep emotions, help them practice calming-down techniques and involve your child in problem-solving.

The most important part is acknowledging your child's efforts and achievements. When they put a lot of effort into managing their emotions, praise their wins, even if it is only a partial win. Encouraging words and displays of support are crucial for your child to continue to learn to be independent and self-regulate their emotions.

Chapter 5: Fostering a Supporting Family Environment

Remote work has significantly benefited our family, especially raising and educating our daughter. As a father, the flexibility to set my own hours and work from home, I've been able to spend more quality time with her, participating in daily learning activities, helping with homework, and even joining virtual classes like piano lessons. This presence has strengthened our bond and allowed us to tailor support to her unique learning style, making her educational experience more personalized and effective. Additionally, remote work has enabled us to create a more balanced family life by managing work around important moments like field trips and extracurricular activities, eliminating the stress of commuting and rigid office hours. This flexibility has fostered a consistent daily routine essential for her development, enhancing our ability to nurture her growth while maintaining a harmonious family environment.

The Importance of Family Dynamics

Even when just one person in the family has traits like attention deficit or hyperactivity, it impacts everybody significantly daily. In a study conducted on 754 families, children aged 7 to 11 were assessed through the Conners Parent Rating Scale, the Haezi Extadi Family Assessment Scale, and The Attention Network Test. It was concluded that family context and attentional control contribute to ADHD symptoms in these children. Also, parental stress and self-efficacy were found to be direct predictors of ADHD symptoms in children of the age group (Barreto-Zarza et al., 2022).

Viewing ADHD as a family-wide endeavor and taking a holistic approach to managing these characteristics of a child in the family will make the child feel understood and supported. A little understanding of what the child is going through and cooperation from all family members will make a pleasant home environment. Educating all family members about their own natural temperaments is very effective. Everyone should know their own strengths and weaknesses for the best family bond. Siblings must cooperate with each other despite their differences. Therefore, it is essential that all their questions are answered and that they are well-informed about the home dynamics so that they do not feel like they are given less attention.

When things like diet, nutrition, exercise, sleep routines, and stress management are dealt with as a family, it becomes easier to manage the symptoms of ADHD in the child.

A positive family dynamic significantly impacts the behavior and emotional well-being of the child. A healthy relationship among family members creates a safe space at home, which will create less stress and uncertainty. When difficult situations like disagreements and small fights happen in the family, siblings, and parents can set an example of how to calm down and resolve the issue with patience. This will encourage the child to adopt the same strategies they have seen when they feel overwhelmed, overstimulated, hyperactive, and in other challenging situations to handle themselves and the problem at hand well.

The family members might find it difficult at times to understand and help them. Therefore, it is advisable to get family therapy, parent training, or join a support group such as a church. It will help to create a healthy home environment for your child and your family.

Open Communication: Strategies for the Whole Family

A home is supposed to be a safe space where we can relax and be without the fear of judgment. Our children should also feel secure at home, able to express their emotions and feelings and speak freely. Your children should openly communicate their excitement and frustrations with you. Creating an environment at home that strengthens family bonds and promotes open communication is essential. Good communication and a stress-free environment are the keys to creating a safe space at home. Discuss the impacts of ADHD and temperament traits with your family. When explaining how to act and respond in difficult situations to your children, speak in a way they can understand. Give examples, play out fake scenarios, and demonstrate the strategies to minimize triggers and handle situations.

All family members should get together at least once daily and share their day. A family dinner can be used to express concerns and share achievements. Ask your children how their day was, what happened at school, and how things are with their friends, and share with them and your spouse any important things that happened with you that day. Make it a point to have family time where everyone feels comfortable expressing their views and sharing their feelings and successes. When your child is speaking, you must listen actively. Active listening is a crucial part of effective communication. Listen to their concerns, be empathetic, make suggestions, and offer a shoulder to lean on or a hug if that's what they need. When they share their achievements, appreciate it and celebrate as a family. Follow active listening with everyone so that each family member feels heard and understood. How you interact with your spouse will also show your kids how they need to behave. Children learn by watching us. They will adopt what they see.

Sibling Dynamics: Fostering Understanding and Support

When there is a child with ADHD or with challenging temperament traits in the family, parents tend to give more attention to them, which is often essential. This might make their siblings feel like they are not getting enough attention and even feel less loved. You must ensure that all your children get equal positive parental attention. Keep things fair when dealing with things in the family, like when creating a reward system for your challenge child for doing complex tasks; do the same for your other kids, too. Make them feel included.

When your difficult child throws a tantrum or has a meltdown, never label them as bad and their siblings as good. This will create sibling rivalry. The child with ADHD will feel less valued, and you might put their sibling in a difficult position. Siblings also feel pressured to be the "good kid" when their parents struggle with their siblings. They feel it is on them to make you feel better, and they should always behave. They put pressure on themselves so as not to cause any familial stress. Studies have shown that siblings of children with characteristics of ADHD often have feelings of shame and guilt—embarrassment when their siblings have a meltdown in public and guilt over the things that come easily to them but their siblings struggle with.

Parents should talk with them and educate them about why their siblings are different, how they can work together as a family, and most importantly, that it is nobody's fault. They have nothing to feel guilty about.

Let them know they are as valuable and loved as their sibling, and they don't have to work extra hard to earn love or keep the family peace.

Talk with your child and discuss the positive roles they can play in supporting their sibling with ADHD or a difficult temperament. Encourage them to help out their sibling when they struggle to complete a task. They can become their confidant and co-adventurer, which will help them strengthen their sibling bond. Include your challenging child in the discussion and give them activities and tasks they can do together. It will help them understand each other, and they will feel like they are getting the fair amount of parental attention they deserve.

Creating Shared Family Goals and Values

Everyone should have an individual goal in life. However, having a shared family goal will strengthen family bonds. Everyone's area of interest should be considered when choosing a family goal. Areas to set a goal could include family health, learning and education, relationship goals, financial goals, or helping others.

Family health goals can include a nighttime routine for better sleep, creating a healthy meal together for better nutrition, having a family physical activity once a week, dividing household chores, or limiting screen time.

The family relationship goals can be family activities, weekend adventures, or working on a home project.

Family learning goals can be reading together every night, learning a new language, taking family field trips, or teaching children to cook and do household chores.

Other things that can be added to family goals include creating a family piggy bank for the next vacation, doing volunteer work as a family, or creating and maintaining a vegetable garden.

To decide on a family goal, first select an area of interest that everyone agrees on and is attainable. This can be done by asking three simple questions:

- What will make our family better?

- What do we aspire to do less or more of?

- What do we want to achieve together as a family?

After you have narrowed down your overall goal, write it down as per the SMART (Specific, Measurable, Achievable, Relevant, Time-bound) goal framework.

- Specific: Specify your goal using the who, what, when, and why questions.

- Measurable: How will the success be measured? For example, how much time spent reading will be considered a success, or how many times does a task need to be done to succeed?

- Achievable: It should be a goal that you can actually achieve.

- Relevant: It should be a goal that actually meets your family's needs and values.

- Time-bound: Figure out the time it will take to achieve the goal. Making it a time-bound goal will prevent any lagging.

After you have decided what your end goal is, write down the steps to reach it. Create the pathway—the small goals to achieve to get to the main goal—and display it somewhere every family member can see. Follow up regularly and mark everyone's progress. A visual progress tracker can be made, and colors and stars can be added when a small goal is achieved.

Celebrating every small win in the goal pathway will encourage children to continue working towards the end goal. Small celebrations like a day out, pizza for dinner, or a movie day will reinforce a positive family culture.

Family Activities That Promote Bonding and Understanding

Family activities are excellent ways to strengthen family bonds while learning and having fun. Engaging in trust-building activities will strengthen the family bond, significantly impacting the family dynamic. It is essential to select inclusive activities that everyone enjoys and meet the needs and energy levels of all family members. Ask everyone to give a list of activities that they would like to do. Then, narrow down the list to the few that include everyone's interests and abilities. Consider the needs, energy level, and attention span of your children when selecting the family activity.

Cooking a meal together, doing arts and crafts projects, or playing age-appropriate board games, cards, and puzzles are fun ways to engage every family member. Outdoor activities like a morning jog, gardening, spending the evening at the playground, swimming, or hiking can also be done together.

Family activities can be learning opportunities for the kids. They help them understand each other's strengths and weaknesses. Games and other group activities instill values and encourage helping others. When done with parents, activities like cooking, gardening, or board games teach children coordination, teamwork, acceptance of each other, patience, and forgiveness.

Family traditions are activities done together as a family for a significant period of time. They bring love and strengthen family bonds, creating everlasting memories for our children. Family activities repeated over time will turn into family traditions, and your children may follow them with their own children someday.

Navigating Parental Stress and Self-care

Recognizing Stress

Being a parent takes work. Being a parent to a child with ADHD or a tough temperament traits is even more challenging. Parenting can put a lot of pressure on someone. We want to do our best for our children and try our best to raise them into strong, independent adults. But sometimes, we focus on our children so much that we forget to care for ourselves. If we want to care for our kids in the best way possible, we should be physically and mentally healthy. The first step is recognizing the signs of stress in yourself and acknowledging that you need help. Stress shows up in different ways in different people. Feeling angry, overwhelmed, irritable, anxious, and tired are some ways you can experience stress. When left untreated, stress can build up and lead to burnout.

Burnout is emotional, physical, and mental exhaustion that occurs from prolonged exposure to stressors and emotionally demanding situations. The symptoms of burnout are sleep deprivation or too much sleep, reduced performance, being fatigued most of the time, memory and concentration problems, decision fatigue, muscle tension, loss of empathy, restlessness, frequent headaches, and getting sick more often. If you feel like these symptoms have been occurring more often, you need to take time and do some self-care.

Self-Care Strategies

Self-care can be anything you do to care for your physical, mental, and emotional health. It will reduce anxiety and stress, improve your mood, and enable you to be better parents to your children. There are some self-care techniques you can use to deal with stress.

If you have started getting angry at the smallest of things, then you might be under some stress. When you feel angry, try stepping away and take a few seconds to cool down before reacting. Try breathing exercises: breathe in and out slowly five times. Leave the room for a few minutes to cool down and regain control. When you feel stressed or worried, try breathing techniques to calm down.

Take a deep breath to fill your lungs, then breathe out slowly. Practice this for two to three minutes, counting to five with each inhale and exhale. While doing this, try to listen to your breath to help you focus on your breathing.

Another way to do this is by adding hand movements. Drop your hands below your waist, keeping your palms facing up. As you breathe through your nose, slowly raise your hands and stop inhaling when your hands reach your shoulder level. Then, slowly lower your hands as you breathe out through your mouth. You can count to five in your mind or listen to your breath as you do this, too.

Breathing exercises will help your tense body to loosen up and relax as stress dissipates. You can teach your children these methods to help them calm down when they feel anxious or have a meltdown.

To enhance your self-care routine, consider incorporating activities such as meditation, prayer, regular exercise, or starting a new hobby. Daily walks for sunlight and fresh air can also be revitalizing. Engaging in these practices can help alleviate stress and boost your overall well-being. Remember, taking care of yourself is essential for being able to care for others effectively.

Seeking Support

If you feel like doing it alone is difficult, then try joining a support group for parents of children with ADHD and temperament traits. If it becomes too difficult to cope with through support groups and self-help, consider meeting a trained professional and receiving help.

There are several online general parent support groups and support groups exclusively for parents of children with ADHD that you can join if you can't find one near you. Joining support groups will help you gain knowledge, share your experiences, hear about other parents' stories, and get emotional support from those experiencing the same parenting journey.

Meeting with an expert psychologist is the next step if you cannot cope with the stress alone. Family therapy and parent training for parents of children with ADHD can help a lot. Family therapy done by including your child in the sessions will show more effective parenting methods, teach your family to work as a unit, and improve your child's behavior, all of which will help to reduce parental stress.

Parent training does not include your child in the sessions. In this, the specialist will guide you to bring down your stress by using effective parenting techniques for your child with ADHD and creating a home environment without stressors. You will be taught forms of positive praise, natural consequences, positive parent-child interaction, how to work with your child's teachers, and how to set limits.

When you take care of yourself, you are demonstrating to your children the significance of taking care of one's mental and physical health. They must learn that the health of your mind is as essential as your body. Set an example for them. Take care of your family by taking care of yourself.

Celebrating the Unique Journey of Your Family

Embracing Uniqueness

With ADHD and temperament differences come challenges as well as strengths. You may not resonate with the other parents whose children do not have these conditions, but embracing your and your child's uniqueness is the best way to move forward. Recognize your child's strengths and help them succeed by focusing on their abilities while trying to overcome the obstacles together. Focus on the positive aspects of your parenthood. How much have you grown as an individual and as a parent? How did you overcome nearly impossible situations while being there for your child who relied on you? The resilience you have built over time and the love that blooms each day have shaped you into a stronger, more compassionate individual.

The progress and growth of a child with ADHD or strong temperament traits and their family's journey will not be the same as those of other families. Therefore, documenting your journey through your child's and family photographs, creating a blog, and keeping a journal is an excellent way to celebrate progress and growth.

Keeping a journal to record your child's progress and milestones and how they overcame their struggles will help you focus on the positive side of being their parent. In recording their journey, you also document your parenting journey, which has a story to tell. Sharing your parenting journey with others will resonate with more people than you think. Many parents who do not abide by conventional parenting methods struggle to raise their children. They need a little hope, and your story can inspire them as other's stories have given you strength. Keep documenting and working with other parents on the same journey by helping each other and holding hands when needed.

Make a Difference with Your Review: Unlock the Power of Generosity

"True joy comes from giving to others, not from receiving." - Unknown

People who give selflessly often find greater happiness in their lives. Let's spread that joy together!

Most people decide which books to read based on reviews. By sharing your thoughts, you can assist fellow parents and readers in discovering this helpful guide.

It costs nothing and takes less than a minute but could make a big difference in someone's journey.

To make a difference, simply scan the QR code below and leave a review.

Thank you for your support!

Ghee & Bee

Conclusion

T he most important step to fostering academic success, improved behavior, and stronger family bonds is understanding and accepting the link between ADHD and temperaments. Before concluding that your child has ADHD, determine their temperament type as well as yours. Educate yourself about the different temperament types every person is born with. Identifying your child's temperament type will give you a deeper understanding of their atypical behavior. Further, identifying your own temperament type will make things less complicated because you can tailor your parenting approach according to both of your temperament types. You will be able to focus on your strong suits to improve your parenting skills and help your child work on improving their strengths instead of focusing on their weak points. You can tailor your parenting style to meet your child's needs and create a peaceful home environment conducive to learning for your unique child.

To ensure our unique child can keep up with others and succeed in this competitive world, we as parents must do our best to support their unique needs and requirements. Use positive behavior systems and customized educational approaches at home and in school. Work with their teachers to create a classroom environment for them to thrive like their peers. Family is everything. Maintaining a happy and healthy family dynamic is essential to this journey. Keep the peace and harmony in the household to avoid overstimulation and overwhelming the child. Give your child activities to divert their hyperactiveness to productive things. In doing so, they might discover their future career calling like the famous Olympians and scientists who had the same struggles.

ADHD and different temperaments make each child unique and bring unique strengths and opportunities for growth. They are different from other kids, and that is their superpower. Help them find their powers and guide them in the right direction to use their strengths to create a successful life for themselves.

This book is only the first step in becoming the parent your child needs. Apply the lessons and strategies you have learned here by tailoring them to meet your child's needs and strengths. Tailor-made parenting unique to you and your child is the right approach. Continue to explore more, be more curious, and never stop looking for knowledge that could improve your child's and your family's lives. Keep reading more, talk to other parents, be involved in the community, and keep improvising as the needs and demands of your child change over time.

References

Acar, I. H., Veziroğlu-Çelik, M., Barata, Ö., & Altay, S. (2022). Association between children's temperament and learning behaviors: contribution of relationships with parents and teachers. *Educational Psychology*, *42*(7), 1–20. https://doi.org/10.1080/01443410.2022.2075541

Ackerman, C. (2019, January 5). *Positive reinforcement in psychology*. Positive Psychology. https://positivepsychology.com/positive-reinforcement-psychology/

ADD/ADHD and Sibling Relationships. (2021, December 3). Children's Medical. https://www.npcmc.com/2021/12/03/add-adhd-and-sibling-relationships/

ADHD: How to help your child at home. (2024, February 20). Aboutkidshealth https://www.aboutkidshealth.ca/adhd-how-to-help-your-child-at-home

ADHD UK. (2023, February 13). *The History of ADHD - ADHD UK*. ADHD UK. https://adhduk.co.uk/the-history-of-adhd/

Al-Hendawi, M. (2013). Temperament, school adjustment, and academic achievement: Existing research and future directions. *Educational Review, 65*(2), 177–205. https://doi.org/10.1080/00131911.2011.648371

Allard, L. T., & Hunter, A. (2009). *CSEFEL: Center on the Social and Emotional Foundations for Early Learning*. Vanderbilt.edu. http://csefel.vanderbilt.edu/resources/wwb/wwb23.html

Allport, G. W. (1937). *Personality: A psychological interpretation*. Holt. https://psycnet.apa.org/record/1938-01964-000

Alvord, M., & Halfond, R. (2019, October 24). *How to help children and teens manage their stress*. American Psychological Association. https://www.apa.org/topics/children/stress

American Academy of Pediatrics. (2019). *How to understand your child's temperament*. HealthyChildren.org. https://www.healthychildren.org/English/ages-stages/gradeschool/Pages/How-to-Understand-Your-Childs-Temperament.aspx

American Psychiatric Association. (2000). *Diagnostic and Statistical Manual of Mental Disorders, Fourth Edition* (4th ed., pp. 85–93). American Psychiatric Association.

Ames, H. (2023, May 25). *Online ADHD parent support group*. Hallowell Todaro ADHD Center. https://www.hallowelltodaro.com/online-adhd-parent-support-group

Amy. (2023, September 4). *6+ engaging and interactive activities for kids with ADHD*. Lingokids. https://lingokids.com/blog/posts/6-engaging-and-interactive-activities-for-kids-with-adhd

Angellove. (n.d.). *ADHD: Disorder or temperament variance?* Storywrite. https://storywrite.com/story/7696575-ADHD--Disorder-or-Temperament-Variance--by-angellove

Arif Kamal, Mo., Chomal, N., & Singh, S. (2024). *Designing learning environment for school children having Attention-Deficit/Hyperactivity Disorder*.

Arnold, L. E., Lofthouse, N., & Hurt, E. (2012). Artificial food colors and Attention-Deficit/Hyperactivity Symptoms: Conclusions to dye for. *Neurotherapeutics, 9*(3), 599–609. https://doi.org/10.1007/s13311-012 -0133-x

Ashton, M. C. (2013, January 1). *Chapter 2 - Personality traits and the inventories that measure them* (M. C. Ashton, Ed.). ScienceDirect; Academic Press. https://www.sciencedirect.com/science/article/abs/pii/ B9780124160095000025

Baby's personality: Chess and Thomas' baby temperaments. (n.d.). Ovia-health. https://www.ovuline.com/guide/14076/baby-temperaments

Bagnato, S., Neisworth, J., Salvia, J., & Hunt, F. (n.d.). *Temperament and Atypical Behavior Scale (TABS) assessment tool.* Brookes Publishing. https://products.brookespublishing.com/Temperament-and-Atypi cal-Behavior-Scale-TABS-Assessment-Tool-P526.aspx

Bapat, M., PhD, Bapat, H. M., PhD, psychologist, H. D. (2021, August 4). *10 parental support groups to help your family thrive.* LoveTo-Know. https://www.lovetoknow.com/parenting/parenthood/10-parent al-support-groups-help-your-family-thrive

Barreto-Zarza, F., Sanchez De Miguel, M., Freijo, E., Acha, J., GonzáleZ, L., Rebagliato, M., & Ibarluzea, J. (2022). Family context and ADHD symptoms in middle childhood: An explanatory model. *Journal of Child and Family Studies, 31.* https://www.researchgate.net/publication/357837898_Family_Context _and_ADHD_Symptoms_in_Middle_Childhood_an_Explanatory_M odel/citation/download

BEd, K. P., M. Psych and Nanette Botha. (2023, October 30). *A practical guide to creating visual schedules.* Autism Parenting Magazine. https://w ww.autismparentingmagazine.com/creating-visual-schedules/

Bell, R. Q. (1968). A reinterpretation of the direction of effects in studies of socialization. *Psychological Review, 75*(2), 81–95. https://doi.org/10.1 037/h0025583

Betker, C. (2017). Environmental strategies for managing Attention Deficit Hyperactivity Disorder. *Journal of Childhood & Developmental Disorders, 03*(04). https://doi.org/10.4172/2472-1786.100062

Beurkens, N. (2021, September 27). *A holistic treatment approach for ADHD symptoms.* Nicole Beurkens. https://www.drbeurkens.com/a-ho listic-approach-to-improving-adhd-symptoms-in-children-and-teens/

Bhargava, D. (2015, December 1). *Empowering learners: Differentiating the curriculum for students with ADHD.* Behaviour Help. https://behaviourhelp.com/behaviour-blog/positive-behaviour-support/ empowering-learners-differentiating-the-curriculum-for-students-with-a dhd

Bhutani, P., Gupta, M., Bajaj, G., Ramesh Chandra Deka, Siddhartha Sankar Satapathy, & Suvendra Kumar Ray. (2024). Is the screen time duration affecting children's language development? - A scoping review. *Clinical Epidemiology and Global Health, 25,* 101457–101457. https:// doi.org/10.1016/j.cegh.2023.101457

Birchwood, J., & Daley, D. (2012). Brief report: The impact of Attention Deficit Hyperactivity Disorder (ADHD) symptoms on academic performance in an adolescent community sample. *Journal of Adolescence, 35*(1), 225–231. https://doi.org/10.1016/j.adolescence.2010.08.011

Bornstein, M. H. (2019). *Handbook of parenting.* Routledge.

Bornstein, M. H., & Lamb, M. E. (2002). *Development in infancy.* Psychology Press.

Bosquet Enlow, M., White, M. T., Hails, K., Cabrera, I., & Wright, R. J. (2016). The infant behavior questionnaire-revised: Factor structure in a culturally and sociodemographically diverse sample in the United States. *Infant Behavior and Development, 43,* 24–35. https://doi.org/10.1016/j .infbeh.2016.04.001

Bouchard, M. F., Bellinger, D. C., Wright, R. O., & Weisskopf, M. G. (2010). Attention-Deficit/Hyperactivity Disorder and urinary metabolites of organophosphate pesticides. *PEDIATRICS, 125*(6), e1270–e1277. https://doi.org/10.1542/peds.2009-3058

Bradley, C. (1937). The behavior of children receiving benzedrine. *American Journal of Psychiatry, 94*(3), 577–585. https://doi.org/10.117 6/ajp.94.3.577

Burgert, N. (2021, August 2). *Dear pediatrician: How do you relieve anxiety in children?* Forbes Health. https://www.forbes.com/health/fam ily/relieve-anxiety-in-children/

Burgher, H. (2023, December 1). *Understand, manage children's temperament for a harmonious holiday season.* Iowa State University. https://www.extension.iastate.edu/news/understand-manage-childre ns-temperament-harmonious-holiday-season

Bussing, R., Zima, B. T., Gary, F. A., & Garvan, C. W. (2003). Barriers to detection, help-seeking, and service use for children with ADHD symptoms. *The Journal of Behavioral Health Services & Research, 30*(2), 176–189. https://doi.org/10.1007/bf02289806

Calming and regulating activities for ADHD. (n.d.). Gympanzees. https://www.gympanzees.org/our-services/online-resource-hub /adhd/10-calming-and-regulating-activities-for-adhd

Carey, W. B. (2004). *Understanding your child's temperament.* Xlibris C o r p o r a t i o n . https://books.google.co.in/books?hl=en&lr=&id=f0tWBAuVfrcC&oi= fnd&pg=PA5&dq=how+understanding+a+child%27s+temperament+c an+lead+to+a+more+effective+and+tailored+parenting+approaches&o ts=ZbIyhVVdB-&sig=Mo6NUzJcLGrZV2gmSfSqY1Zdc38#v=onepage &q&f=false

Caspi, A., Harrington, H., Milne, B., Amell, J. W., Theodore, R. F., & Moffitt, T. E. (2003). Children's behavioral styles at age 3 are linked to their adult personality traits at age 26. *Journal of Personality, 71*(4), 495–514. https://doi.org/10.1111/1467-6494.7104001

CECMHC | Infant toddler temperament tool. (n.d.). ECMHC. https://www.ecmhc.org/temperament/

Centers for Disease Control and Prevention. (2023, September 27). *What is ADHD?* Centers for Disease Control and Prevention. https://www.cdc.gov/ncbddd/adhd/facts.html

Challenging behavior as communication. (n.d.). Evidence-Based Instructional Practices. https://ebip.vkcsites.org/challenging-behavior-as-communication/

Changing the environment: Positive behaviour strategy. (2024, April 12). Raising Children Network. https://raisingchildren.net.au/school-age/behaviour/behaviour-management-tips-tools/changing-environment#:~:text=Children%27s%20behaviour%20is%20influenced%20by

Checa, P., & Abundis-Gutierrez, A. (2017). Parenting and temperament influence on school success in 9–13 year olds. *Front. Psychol.* 8:543. https://www.frontiersin.org/journals/psychology/articles/10.3389/fpsyg.2017.00543/full

Chess, S., & Thomas, A. (1995). *Temperament in clinical practice.* Guilford Press. https://books.google.co.in/books/about/Temperament_in_Clinical_Practice.html?id=s3y2tfBq1vQC&redir_esc=y

Chess, S., & Thomas, A. (1986). *The New York Longitudinal Study: From infancy to early adulthood.* Psychology Press.

Chiang, H.-L., Chuang, Y.-F., Chen, Y.-A., Hsu, C.-T., Ho, C.-C., Hsu, H.-T., Sheu, Y.-H., Gau, S. S.-F., & Liang, L.-L. (2024). *Physical fitness and risk of mental disorders in children and adolescents.* JAMA Pediatrics. https://doi.org/10.1001/jamapediatrics.2024.0806

Child temperament, ADHD and caregiver strain: Exploring relationships in an epidemiological sample. (n.d.). *Journal of the American Academy of Child and Adolescent Psychiatry, 42*(2).

Circle of parents. (n.d.). Circle of Parents. http://circleofparents.org

Climie, E. A., & Mitchell, K. (2016). Parent-child relationship and behavior problems in children with ADHD. *International Journal of Developmental Disabilities, 63*(1), 27–35. https://doi.org/10.1080/20473869.2015.1112498

Cloninger, C. (1994). Temperament and personality. *Current Opinion in Neurobiology, 4*(2), 266–273. https://doi.org/10.1016/0959-4388(94)90083-3

Coach, J. A. W. / P. (n.d.). Heartprints: Understand your child's temperament. *Heart Manity.* https://blog.heartmanity.com/heartprints-understand-your-childs-temperament

Common ADHD challenges and characteristics — leaf complex care. (2023, August 3). Leafcare.co.uk. https://leafcare.co.uk/blog/common-adhd-challenges-and-characteristics/

Cooks-Campbell, A. (2022, February 1). *Slow down: How mindful parenting benefits both parents and lids.* Betterup. https://www.betterup.com/blog/mindful-parenting

Correspondents, M. (2024, February 15). *Adapting parenting strategies could mitigate ADHD development in exuberant children: New study reveals.* Medriva. https://medriva.com/adhd/adapting-parenting-strategies-could-mitigate-adhd-development-in-exuberant-children-new-study-reveals/

Cross, J. (2019, August 8). *What does too much screen time do to kids' brains?* Health Matters. https://healthmatters.nyp.org/what-does-too-much-screen-time-do-to-childrens-brains/

Das, T. (2023, December 23). *How to limit screen time for kids: Psychologist shared tips.* Hindustan Times. https://www.hindustantimes.com/lifestyle/health/how-to-limit-screen-time-for-kids-psychologist-shared-tips-101703310732363.html

Dawson, P. (2023, October 30). *Strategies to make homework go more smoothly.* Child Mind Institute. https://childmind.org/article/strategies-to-make-homework-go-more-smoothly/

Day, N. (2023, April 20). *Differentiation in the classroom: Key tips to meet the needs of every student.* Raising an Extraordinary Person. https://hes-extraordinary.com/differentiation-in-the-classroom

Drechsler, R., Brem, S., Brandeis, D., Grublatt, E., Berger, G., & Walitza,S. (2020, October). ADHD: Current Concepts and Treatments in Children and Adolescents. *Neuropediatrics,* vol. 51, no. 5, pp. 315–335. https://pubmed.ncbi.nlm.nih.gov/32559806/

E. Brown, T. (2023, September 28). *Complexity of ADHD with comorbid disorders webinar.* Pearson Assessments. https://www.pearsonassessments.com/professional-assessments/blog-we binars/webinars/2023/09/complexity-of-adhd-with-comorbid-disorders -webinar.html#:~:text=Increasingly%20ADHD%20has%20been%20reco gnized

Early warning signs of ADHD. (2015, November 21). Healthy Children. https://www.healthychildren.org/English/health-issues/condition s/adhd/Pages/Early-Warning-Signs-of-ADHD.aspx

Elksnin, L. K. (2005). Temperament in the classroom: Understanding individual differences. *Psychology in the Schools, 42*(2), 223–224. https://doi.org/10.1002/pits.20060

EuroKids. (2023, September 29). *Child temperament: Characteristics, types, and management strategies.* EuroKids. https://www.eurokidsindia.com/blog/understanding-child-temperamen t-characteristics-varieties-and-strategies-for-effective-management.php

Farrington, D. P., & Jolliffe, D. (2001, January 1). *Personality and crime.* Science Direct. https://www.sciencedirect.com/science/article/abs/pii/B 0080430767017800

Flynn, L. (2022, August 8). *Effective visual schedules for ADHD.* OT4ADHD. https://ot4adhd.com/2022/08/08/effective-visual-schedul es-for-adhd/

Folaron, G. (2024, January 23). *ADHD in project management: Harnessing strengths & challenges*. Leantime. https://leantime.io/adhd-and-project-management-the-good-and-bad/

Foley, M., McClowry, S. G., & Castellanos, F. X. (2008). The relationship between attention deficit hyperactivity disorder and child temperament. *Journal of Applied Developmental Psychology, 29*(2), 157–169. https://doi.org/10.1016/j.appdev.2007.12.005

Fortunato, A., Tanzilli, A., Lingiardi, V., & Speranza, A. M. (2021). Childhood Personality Assessment Q-Sort (CPAP-Q): A clinically and empirically procedure for assessing traits and emerging patterns of personality in childhood. *International Journal of Environmental Research and Public Health, 18*(12), 6288. https://doi.org/10.3390/ijerph18126288

Fowler, G. A., & Hunter, T. (2024, February 2). Expert strategies that (really) help kids reduce screen time. *Washington Post*. https://www.washingtonpost.com/technology/2024/01/26/how-to-reduce-screen-time-kids/

Fullard, W., McDevitt, S. C., & Carey, W. B. (1984). Assessing temperament in one-to three-year-old children. *Journal of Pediatric Psychology, 9*(2), 205–217. https://doi.org/10.1093/jpepsy/9.2.205

Garey, J. (2024, March 9). *Getting family members on board with treatment*. Child Mind Institute. https://childmind.org/article/getting-family-members-on-board-with-treatment/

Gartstein, M. A., & Rothbart, M. K. (2003). Studying infant temperament via the Revised Infant Behavior Questionnaire. *Infant Behavior and Development, 26*(1), 64–86. https://doi.org/10.1016/s0163-6383(02)00169-8

Ghosh, S. (2023, January 7). Personalized approach to child development - Indian parenting styles. UpTodd. https://www.uptodd.com/blog/indian-parenting-personalized-child-development

Gill, K. (2023, June 1). *ADHD diet for kids: Which foods can help and which to avoid.* Medical News Today. https://www.medicalnewstoday.com/articles/adhd-diet-for-kids

Gillette, H. (2024, March 14). *24 activities for children with ADHD.* Healthline. https://www.healthline.com/health/adhd/activities-for-children-with-adhd#24-activities

Goldsmith, H., & Rothbart, M. (1991, January). *Contemporary instruments for assessing early temperament by questionnaire and in the l a b o r a t o r y .* https://www.researchgate.net/publication/279410080_Contemporary_Instruments_for_Assessing_Early_Temperament_by_Questionnaire_and_in_the_Laboratory

Goswami, P., & Parekh, V. (2024). The impact of screen time on child and adolescent development: A review. *International Journal of Contemporary Pediatrics.* https://dx.doi.org/10.18203/2349-3291.ijcp20231865

Gracias, A. (2018, February 22). *Child's temperament: Finding the right parenting style to match it.* Parent Circle. https://www.parentcircle.com/finding-the-right-parenting-style-to-match-children-temperament/article

Gregory, L. (2022, December 6). *Anecdotal record: Child observation tool for early educators.* My Bright Wheel. https://mybrightwheel.com/blog/anecdotal-record

Guyer, A. E., Jarcho, J. M., Pérez-Edgar, K., Degnan, K. A., Pine, D. S., Fox, N. A., & Nelson, E. E. (2015). Temperament and parenting styles in early childhood differentially influence neural response to peer evaluation in adolescence. *Journal of Abnormal Child Psychology, 43*(5), 863–874. https://doi.org/10.1007/s10802-015-9973-2

Hallowell, E. (2021, May 6). *12 ways to build strong ADHD relationships in families.* Additudemag. https://www.additudemag.com/12-ways-to-build-strong-add-families/

Harpin, V. A. (2005). The effect of ADHD on the life of an individual, their family, and community from preschool to adult Life. *Archives of Disease in Childhood, 90*(1), i2–i7. https://doi.org/10.1136/adc.2004.059006

Hasan, S. (2017). *Parenting a child with ADHD (for parents).* Kids Health. https://kidshealth.org/en/parents/parenting-kid-adhd.html

Hayden, E. P., Klein, D. N., & Durbin, C. E. (2005). Parent reports and laboratory assessments of child temperament: A comparison of their associations with risk for depression and externalizing disorders. *Journal of Psychopathology and Behavioral Assessment, 27*(2), 89–100. https://doi.org/10.1007/s10862-005-5383-z

Hei Schools. (2022, March 28). *What is holistic development?* Heischools. https://www.heischools.com/blog/what-is-holistic-development

How can I support a child with ADHD at home? (n.d.). Support for Parents from Action for Children. https://parents.actionforchildren.org.uk/development-additional-needs/neurodiversity/support-child-adhd/

How to reduce stress. (n.d.). UNICEF. https://www.unicef.org/parenting/mental-health/how-reduce-stress-parents

Huerta, M. (2015, January 22). *Meeting the needs of students with ADHD.* Edutopia. https://www.edutopia.org/blog/bridging-the-adhd-gap-merle-huerta

Interactive, B. R. (2021, March 27). *ADHD impact different life stages.* IPC. https://www.ipc-mn.com/what-impact-does-adhd-have-at-different-stages-of-life/

IT3: More about this tool. (2020, March 18). ECLKC. https://eclkc.ohs.acf.hhs.gov/mental-health/article/it3-more-about-tool

J. Legg, T. (2015). *6 natural remedies for ADHD, triggers to avoid, and more.* Healthline. https://www.healthline.com/health/adhd/natural-remedies

Jansen, E. (n.d.). *Cracking the code: Revealing the best psychological assessment tools for children.* Quenza. https://quenza.com/blog/knowledge-base/psychological-assessment-tools-for-children/

Jordan, C. (2022, May 10). *Proceed with caution: 10 things you should consider before stopping your ADHD meds.* WebMD. https://www.webmd.com/add-adhd/ss/cm/10-things-you-should-consider-before-stopping-adhd-meds

K Rothbart, M. (2019, February). *Temperament.* Encyclopedia on Early Childhood Development. https://www.child-encyclopedia.com/temperament/according-experts/early-temperament-and-psychosocial-development

Keogh, B. (2023, February 6). *Temperament in the classroom: Helping each child find a good fit.* Parenting. https://www.greatschools.org/gk/articles/temperament-in-the-classroom-helping-each-child-find-a-good-fit/

Kennedy, L. (2022, January 14). *28 examples of family goals to achieve this year.* Prodigy Game. https://www.prodigygame.com/main-en/blog/family-goals/

Kiff, C. J., Lengua, L. J., & Zalewski, M. (2011). Nature and nurturing: Parenting in the context of child temperament. *Clinical Child and Family Psychology Review, 14*(3), 251–301. https://doi.org/10.1007/s10567-011-0093-4

King, K., Alexander, D., & Seabi, J. (2016). Siblings' perceptions of their ADHD-diagnosed sibling's impact on the family system. *International Journal of Environmental Research and Public Health, 13*(9), 910. https://doi.org/10.3390/ijerph13090910

Klass, P., & M.D. (2018, April 23). Helping kids with A.D.H.D., and their families, thrive. *The New York Times.* https://www.nytimes.com/2018/04/23/well/family/helping-kids-with-adhd-and-their-families-thrive.html

Konke, L. A., Forslund, T., Nilsson-Jobs, E., Nyström, P., Falck-Ytter, T., & Brocki, K. (2021). How does temperament in toddlers at elevated likelihood for autism relate to symptoms of autism and ADHD at three years of age? *Journal of Autism and Developmental Disorders, 52*. https://doi.org/10.1007/s10803-021-05001-z

Kopko, K. (2007, August 21). *Child development and the physical environment*. HD Today. https://hdtoday.human.cornell.edu/2007/08/21/child-development-and-the-physical-environment/

Kos, J. M., & Richdale, A. L. (2004). The history of attention-deficit/hyperactivity disorder. *Australian Journal of Learning Disabilities, 9*(1), 22–24. https://doi.org/10.1080/19404150409546751

Koseva, N. (2022, October 28). *How does ADHD affect children's behaviour?* The ADHD Centre. https://www.adhdcentre.co.uk/how-does-adhd-affect-childrens-behaviour/

Krieger, V., Amador-Campos, J. A., & Gallardo-Pujol, D. (2019). Temperament, executive function, and attention-deficit/hyperactivity disorder (ADHD) in adolescents: The mediating role of effortful control. *Journal of Clinical and Experimental Neuropsychology, 41*(6), 615–633. https://doi.org/10.1080/13803395.2019.1599824

Krishnan, S. (2021, December 9). Tips on parenting children with ADHD. *The Times of India*. https://timesofindia.indiatimes.com/readersblog/be-best/tips-on-parenting-children-with-adhd-39496/

Kumar, S. (2020, September 14). *How does social environment impacts child's behavior?* Times of India Blog. https://timesofindia.indiatimes.com/readersblog/sawan/how-does-social-environment-impacts-childs-behavior-26029/

Kuriyama, S., Metoki, H., Kikuya, M., Obara, T., Ishikuro, M., Yamanaka, C., Nagai, M., Matsubara, H., Kobayashi, T., Sugawara, J., Tamiya, G., Hozawa, A., Nakaya, N., Tsuchiya, N., Nakamura, T., Narita, A., Kogure, M., Hirata, T., Tsuji, I., & Nagami, F. (2019). Cohort Profile: Tohoku Medical Megabank Project Birth and Three-Generation Cohort Study (TMM BirThree Cohort Study): Rationale, progress and perspective. *International Journal of Epidemiology, 49*(1). https://doi.org/10.10 93/ije/dyz169

Kusumasari, D., Junaedi, D., & Kaburuan, E. R. (2018). Designing an interactive learning application for ADHD children. *MATEC Web of Conferences, 197*, 16008. https://doi.org/10.1051/matecconf/20181971 6008

L'Estrange, L. (2017, December 6). *Understanding A child's meltdown.* Hand in Hand Parenting. https://www.handinhandparenting.org/2017 /12/understanding-childrens-meltdowns/

Lange, K. W., Reichl, S., Lange, K. M., Tucha, L., & Tucha, O. (2010). The history of attention deficit hyperactivity disorder. *ADHD Attention Deficit and Hyperactivity Disorders, 2*(4), 241–255. https://doi.org/10.1 007/s12402-010-0045-8

Learning differences in history: Leonardo da Vinci to Muhammad Ali. (2019, August 5). Understood. https://www.understood.org/en/articles /historical-figures-who-may-have-had-learning-and-thinking-differences

Lebrun-Harris, L. A., Ghandour, R. M., Kogan, M. D., & Warren, M. D. (2022). Five-year trends in US children's health and well-being, 2016-2020. *JAMA Pediatrics, 176*(7), 1–11. https://doi.org/10.1001/ja mapediatrics.2022.0056

Lesser, J. (2022, June 14). *Sibling rivalry: ADHD family dynamics, positive parenting & more.* Additudemag. https://www.additudemag.co m/sibling-rivalry-adhd-positive-parenting-tips/

Lewien, C., Genuneit, J., Meigen, C., Kiess, W., & Poulain, T. (2021). Sleep-related difficulties in healthy children and adolescents. *BMC Pediatrics, 21*(1). https://doi.org/10.1186/s12887-021-02529-y

Li, M., & Pang, K. (2007). A study on the relationship between temperament and mathematics academic achievement. *Research in Mathematical Education, 11*(3), 197–207.

Lorenzo, N. E., Hong N.T. Bui, Degnan, K. A., McDermott, J. M., Henderson, H. A., Fox, N. A., & Chronis-Tuscano, A. (2023). The developmental unfolding of ADHD symptoms from early childhood through adolescence: Early effects of exuberant temperament, parenting and executive functioning. *Research on Child and Adolescent Psychopathology.* https://doi.org/10.1007/s10802-023-01140-2

Low, K. (2022, April 19). *Why children with ADHD need structure and routines.* Verywell Mind. https://www.verywellmind.com/why-is-structure-important-for-kids-with-adhd-20747

M. Hennessey, J. (2015). *Interaction effects of parenting styles and child temperament: Motor, cognitive, and language development in children prenatally exposed to alcohol.* Duquesne University. https://core.ac.uk/download/pdf/234047252.pdf

Matheny, A. P., Wilson, R. S., & Thoben, A. S. (1987). Home and mother: Relations with infant temperament. *Developmental Psychology, 23*(3), 323–331. https://doi.org/10.1037/0012-1649.23.3.323

Martinez-Badía, J. (2015). Who says this is a modern disorder? The early history of attention deficit hyperactivity disorder. *World Journal of Psychiatry, 5*(4), 379–386. https://doi.org/10.5498/wjp.v5.i4.379

Marvin, H. (2024, January 24). Strengthening family ties: Simple activities for cultivating trust and unity. *Satchel Pulse.* https://blog.satchelpulse.com/strengthening-family-ties-simple-activities-for-cultivating-trust-and-unity

McClowry, S. G. (1995). The development of the school-age temperament inventory. *Merrill-Palmer Quarterly: Journal of Developmental Psychology, 41*(3). https://psycnet.apa.org/record/1995-42412-001

McClowry, S. G. (1998). The science and art of using temperament as the basis for intervention. *School Psychology Review, 27*(4), 551–563. https://doi.org/10.1080/02796015.1998.12085937

McClowry, S. G. (2002). The temperament profiles of school-age children. *Journal of Pediatric Nursing, 17*(1), 3–10. https://doi.org/10.1053/jpdn.2002.30929

McGillivray, C. (2024, January 11). *What is "parent training" for families of children with ADHD?* The Conversation. https://theconversation.com/what-is-parent-training-for-families-of-children-with-adhd-217381

McIntosh, D. E., & Cole-Love, A. S. (1996). Profile comparisons between ADHD and non-ADHD children on the temperament assessment battery for children. *Journal of Psychoeducational Assessment, 14*(4), 362–372. https://doi.org/10.1177/073428299601400404

Mcleod, S. (2024). Maslow's hierarchy of needs. *Simply Psychology, 1*(1-18). https://www.simplypsychology.org/maslow.html?ez_vid=2cae626a2fe896279da43d587baa3eb663083817

McQueen, J. (2022, May 27). *Family therapy for childhood ADHD: What to know.* WebMD. https://www.webmd.com/add-adhd/childhood-adhd/childhood-adhd-family-therapy

Miller, C. (2016, February 25). *Why do kids have tantrums and meltdowns?* Child Mind Institute. https://childmind.org/article/why-do-kids-have-tantrums-and-meltdowns/

Mindful parenting: what it is, benefits & 10 ways to practice. (2024, April 5). *Calm Blog.* https://www.calm.com/blog/mindful-parenting

Montejo, J. E., Durán, M., del Mar Martínez, M., Hilari, A., Roncalli, N., Vilaregut, A., Corrales, M., Nogueira, M., Casas, M., Linares, J. L., & Ramos-Quiroga, J. A. (2015). Family functioning and parental bonding during childhood in adults diagnosed With ADHD. *Journal of Attention Disorders, 23*(1), 57–64. https://doi.org/10.1177/1087054715596578

More inclusive activities to encourage your children to play. (n.d.). She Heroes. https://sheheroes.org/more-inclusive-activities-to-encourage-your-children-to-play/

Morin, A. (n.d.). *Taming tantrums vs. managing meltdowns.* Understood. https://www.understood.org/en/articles/taming-tantrums-vs-managing-meltdowns#:~:text=Meltdowns%20are%20a%20full%2Dbody

Morin, A. (2013, July 2). *10 ways to limit your child's screen time.* Verywell Family. https://www.verywellfamily.com/tips-for-limiting-electronics-and-screen-time-for-kids-1094870

Morin, A. (2022a). *Accommodations to help students with ADD and ADHD.* Understood. https://www.understood.org/en/articles/classroom-accommodations-for-adhd

Morin, A. (2022b, January 18). *How to tailor your discipline to meet your child's needs.* Verywell Family. https://www.verywellfamily.com/how-to-tailor-discipline-to-your-childs-temperament-1094786

Morin, A. (2024, April 16). *How positive reinforcement encourages good behavior in kids.* Parents. https://www.parents.com/positive-reinforcement-examples-8619283#:~:text=Using%20Positive%20Reinforcement%20To%20Reward

Mulligan, S. (2001). Classroom strategies used by teachers of students with Attention Deficit Hyperactivity Disorder. *Physical & Occupational Therapy in Pediatrics, 20*(4), 25–44. https://doi.org/10.1080/j006v20n04_03

Muppalla, S. K., Vuppalapati, S., Pulliahgaru, A. R., & Sreenivasulu, H. (2023). Effects of excessive screen time on child development: An updated review and strategies for management. *Cureus, 15*(6). https://doi.org/10.7759/cureus.40608

Muris, P., & Ollendick, T. H. (2005). The role of temperament in the etiology of child psychopathology. *Clinical Child and Family Psychology Review, 8*(4), 271–289. https://doi.org/10.1007/s10567-005-8809-y

Nasvytienė, D., & Lazdauskas, T. (2021). Temperament and academic achievement in children: A meta-analysis. *European Journal of Investigation in Health, Psychology and Education, 11*(3), 736–757. https://doi.org/10.3390/ejihpe11030053

National Institute of Mental Health. (2023, September). *Attention-Deficit/Hyperactivity Disorder.* National Institute of Mental

Health. https://www.nimh.nih.gov/health/topics/attention-deficit-hyperactivity-disorder-adhd

Nelson, C. (2020). *Babies need humans, not screens.* Unicef. https://www.unicef.org/parenting/child-development/babies-screen-time

Newcorn, J. H., Weiss, M., & Stein, M. A. (2007). The complexity of ADHD: diagnosis and treatment of the adult patient with comorbidities. *CNS Spectrums, 12*(S12), 1–16. https://doi.org/10.1017/s1092852900026158

Nigg, J. T. (2022). Parsing ADHD with temperament traits. *Current Directions in Psychological Science, 31*(4), 324–332. https://doi.org/10.1177/09637214221098079

Novotni, M., & Ph.D. (2007, July 10). *No judgment. No guilt. Just ADHD support and understanding.* ADDitude. https://www.additudemag.com/youre-not-alone/

Oakland, T., & Joyce, D. (2004). Temperament-based learning styles and school-based applications. *Canadian Journal of School Psychology, 19*(1-2), 59–74. https://doi.org/10.1177/082957350401900103

O'Malley, E. (2023, June 12). *Learning in school and for life: A holistic approach to child development.* Global Partnership for Education. https://www.globalpartnership.org/blog/learning-school-and-life-holistic-approach-child-development

OSEP Director speaks to behavior as a form of communication. (2023, April 25). Individuals with Disabilities Education Act. https://sites.ed.gov/idea/behavior-as-a-form-of-communication/

Ostergren, C. S. (1997). Differential utility of temperament-based guidance materials for parents of infants. *Family Relations, 46*(1), 63. https://doi.org/10.2307/585608

Özyürek, A., Kahraman, Ö., & Pekdoğan, S. (2020). Issue 7 Ser. I. *International Journal of Humanities and Social Science Invention (IJHSSI), 9*(7), 5–12. https://doi.org/10.35629/7722-0907010512

Pahlavanzadeh, S., Mousavi, S., & Maghsoudi, J. (2018). Exploring the needs of family caregivers of children with Attention Deficit Hyperactivity Disorder: A qualitative study. *Iranian Journal of Nursing and Midwifery Research, 23*(2), 149–154. https://doi.org/10.4103/ijnmr.IJNMR_16_17

Pandey, S. (2022, July 8). *What is a meltdown? Why kids be melting down?* VEDANTU. https://www.vedantu.com/blog/reasons-for-kids-meltdown

Pappas, S. (2020, April 1). What do we really know about kids and screens? *American Psychological Association*, 42. https://www.apa.org/monitor/2020/04/cover-kids-screens

Parenting a child with ADHD. (n.d.). Goranson Bain Ausley. https://gbfamilylaw.com/a-familys-guide-to-parenting-a-child-with-adhd/

Patterson, J. (2023, November 14). *ADHD family dynamics: Dealing with difficult family members*. ADDitudemag. https://www.additudemag.com/family-dynamics-adhd-difficult-relatives/

Peasgood, T., Bhardwaj, A., Biggs, K., Brazier, J. E., Coghill, D., Cooper, C. L., Daley, D., De Silva, C., Harpin, V., Hodgkins, P., Nadkarni, A., Setyawan, J., & Sonuga-Barke, E. J. S. (2016). The impact of ADHD on the health and well-being of ADHD children and their siblings. *European Child & Adolescent Psychiatry, 25*(11), 1217–1231. https://doi.org/10.1007/s00787-016-0841-6

Perry, E. (2024, January 2). *20 family goals examples to share with your loved ones*. Better Up. https://www.betterup.com/blog/family-goals

Personalised parenting support. (2016, January). LinkedIn. https://www.linkedin.com/pulse/personalised-parenting-support-diane-parnham/

Peterson, G., & Elam, E. (2020). *Observation and assessment in early childhood education*. NSCC. https://pressbooks.nscc.ca/ece-observation/

Ph.D, D. D. (2022, February 3). *A new approach to parenting*. Elemental. https://elemental.medium.com/a-new-approach-to-parenting-ef77cc078e70

Pinto, S., Correia-de-Sá, T., Sampaio-Maia, B., Vasconcelos, C., Moreira, P., & Ferreira-Gomes, J. (2022). Eating patterns and dietary interventions in ADHD: A narrative review. *Nutrients, 14*(20), 4332. https://do i.org/10.3390/nu14204332

Place2Be. (2021, April 9). *Looking behind the behaviour – how children communicate.* Place2Be. https://www.place2be.org.uk/about-us/news-and-blogs/2021 /april/looking-behind-the-behaviour-how-children-communicate/

Plomin, R., & Dunn, J. (2013). *The study of temperament.* Psychology Press.

Pomfret, H. (2023, October 30). *The science behind your child's tantrums.* Anchor Light Therapy Collective. https://anchorlighttherap y.com/the-science-behind-your-childs-tantrums/

Ponti, M., Bélanger, S., Grimes, R., Heard, J., Johnson, M., Moreau, E., Norris, M., Shaw, A., Stanwick, R., Van Lankveld, J., & Williams, R. (2017). Screen time and young children: Promoting health and development in a digital world. *Paediatrics & Child Health, 22*(8), 461–468. https://doi.org/10.1093/pch/pxx123

Porter, E. (2017, October 13). *Parenting tips for ADHD: Do's and don'ts.* Healthline. https://www.healthline.com/health/adhd/parenting -tips#behavior-management

Potmesilova, P., & Potmesil, M. (2021). Temperament and school readiness – A literature review. *Frontiers in Psychology, 12.* https://doi.org/10 .3389/fpsyg.2021.599411

Psychology, H. (2023, October 11). *Unlocking potential: Personalized education for children with ADHD.* Herrera Psychology. https://herrera psychology.com/personalized-education-for-children-with-adhd/

PsyD, A. O. (2024, February 4). *A temperament-informed approach for effective parenting for children with ADHD.* Medium. https://medium.com/@akiraolsen/a-temperament-informed-appro ach-for-effective-parenting-for-children-with-adhd-35211f9c30e9

Putnam, S., Sanson, A., & Rothbart, M. (2002). Child temperament and parenting. *Handbook of Parenting, 1*, 255–277.

Raising children. (2017, November 2). *Temperament: what it is and why it matters*. Raising Children Network. https://raisingchildren.net.au/ne wborns/behaviour/understanding-behaviour/temperament

R. Remata, H., & S. Lomibao, L. (2021). Attention Deficit Hyperactivity Disorder (ADHD). *American Journal of Educational Research, 9*(7), 426–430. https://doi.org/10.12691/education-9-7-5

Rettew, D. C., & McKee, L. (2005). Temperament and it's role in developmental psychopathology. *Harvard Review of Psychiatry, 13*(1), 14–27. https://doi.org/10.1080/10673220590923146

Reuben, Cynthia, and Nazik Elgaddal. (2024, March). Attention-Deficit/Hyperactivity Disorder in children ages 5-17 years: United States, 2020-2022. *NCHS Data Brief* (499):1-9. https://pubmed.ncbi.nl m.nih.gov/38536951/

Robbins, J. (2020, January 9). *Ecopsychology: How immersion in nature benefits your health*. Yale School of Environment. https://e360.yale.edu/f eatures/ecopsychology-how-immersion-in-nature-benefits-your-health

Rodriguez-Cayro, K. (2023, March 16). 6 personality traits that may secretly be ADHD. *HuffPost*. https://www.huffpost.com/entry/habits-a dhd_l_6408af64e4b0c62918dffeab

Rogers, K. (2023, August 21). *Screen time linked with developmental delays, study finds*. CNN. https://edition.cnn.com/2023/08/21/health/ screen-time-child-development-delays-risks-wellness/index.html

Rothbart, M. K. (1981). Measurement of temperament in infancy. *Child Development, 52*(2), 569–578. https://doi.org/10.2307/1129176

Rothbart, M. K. (1989). Temperament and development. *Temperament in Childhood* (pp. 187–248). https://psycnet.apa.org/record/1990-9727 1-012

Rothbart, M. K., & Bates, J. (2006). Temperament. *Handbook of child psychology: Social, emotional, and personality development* (Vol. 3, pp. 99–166). https://psycnet.apa.org/record/2006-08776-003

Roy, A., Garner, A. A., Epstein, J. N., Hoza, B., Nichols, J. Q., Molina, B. S. G., Swanson, J. M., Arnold, L. E., & Hechtman, L. (2020). Effects of childhood and adult persistent Attention-Deficit/Hyperactivity Disorder on risk of motor vehicle crashes: Results from the multimodal treatment study of children with Attention-Deficit/Hyperactivity Disorder. *Journal of the American Academy of Child & Adolescent Psychiatry, 59*(8), 952–963. https://doi.org/10.1016/j.jaac.2019.08.007

Rutter, M. (1987). Psychosocial resilience and protective mechanisms. *American Journal of Orthopsychiatry, 57*(3), 316–331. https://doi.org/1 0.1111/j.1939-0025.1987.tb03541.x

S, Newmark, y, & M.D. (2020, October 13). *The big 3: How nutrition, exercise & sleep curb ADHD in children.* ADDitude. https://www.addit udemag.com/natural-remedies-adhd-children-nutrition-exercise-sleep/

Sanders, M. R., & Mazzucchelli, T. G. (2013). The promotion of self-regulation through parenting interventions. *Clinical Child and Family Psychology Review, 16*(1), 1–17. https://doi.org/10.1007/s10567-013 -0129-z

Sanson, A., Hemphill, S. A., & Smart, D. (2004). Connections between temperament and social development: A review. *Social Development, 13*(1), 142–170. https://doi.org/10.1046/j.1467-9507.2004.0026 1.x

Saps, M., Seshadri, R., Sztainberg, M., Schaffer, G., Marshall, B. M., & Di Lorenzo, C. (2009). A prospective school-based study of abdominal pain and other common somatic complaints in children. *The Journal of Pediatrics, 154*(3), 322–326. https://doi.org/10.1016/j.jpeds.2008.09.0 47

Scarlet. (2022, September 21). *How to establish a homework routine.* Family Focus Blog. https://familyfocusblog.com/5-homework-tips-pare nts-restless-kids/

Schulze, S. (2023, May 18). *How to create the best school environment for ADHD students.* Joonapp.io. https://www.joonapp.io/post/best-school-environment-for-adhd#:~:text =Changes%20to%20the%20environment%20to%20limit%20distraction &text=Seating%20arrangements%20can%20also%20help

Screen-free family bonding activities. (2024). Twinkl.co.in. https://ww w.twinkl.co.in/resource/screen-free-family-bonding-activities-t-p-3282

Sealy, M. A., Rudasill, K. M., Barrett, J. S., Eum, J., Adams, N., Hin- richs, A., & McClowry, S. (2021). *Temperament in the early elementary classroom: Implications for practice.* IntechOpen. https://www.intechope n.com/chapters/75400

Shah, R., Chauhan, N., Padhy, S., & Malhotra, S. (2019). Relation between temperament dimensions and Attention-Deficit/Hyperactivity Disorder symptoms. *Industrial Psychiatry Journal, 28*(1), 58. https://do i.org/10.4103/ipj.ipj_74_19

Siegel, V. (2006, October 6). *Two Ws and an H: Establishing a homework routine.* ADDitude. https://www.additudemag.com/homework-routin es/

Sleep problems in children. (2022, November 14). WebMD. https://w ww.webmd.com/sleep-disorders/children-sleep-problems

Smith, M., Robinson, L., & Segal, J. (2019, January 10). *ADHD in children.* HelpGuide. https://www.helpguide.org/articles/add-adhd/att ention-deficit-disorder-adhd-in-children.htm

Smith, M., & Segal, J. (2019). *Teaching students with ADHD.* HelpGuide. https://www.helpguide.org/articles/add-adhd/teaching-stu dents-with-adhd-attention-deficit-disorder.htm

Stifter, C. A., Willoughby, M. T., & Towe-Goodman, N. (2008). Agree or agree to disagree? Assessing the convergence between parents and observers on infant temperament. *Infant and Child Development, 17*(4), 407–426. https://doi.org/10.1002/icd.584

Stephens, K. (n.d.) *Strategies for parenting children with difficult temperament.* Parenting Exchange. https://exchangepress.com/library_pe/5 235002.pdf

Stress busting activities for young children. (n.d.). PennState Extension. https://extension.psu.edu/programs/betterkidcare/content-areas/enviro nment-curriculum/activities/all-activities/stress-busting-activities-for-yo ung-children

Summer, J. (2022, April 28). *Sleep disorders in children.* Sleep Foundation. https://www.sleepfoundation.org/children-and-sleep/sleep-diso rders-in-children

Takahashi, I., Obara, T., Ishikuro, M., Murakami, K., Ueno, F., Noda, A., Onuma, T., Shinoda, G., Nishimura, T., Tsuchiya, K. J., & Kuriyama, S. (2023). Screen time at age 1 year and communication and problem-solving developmental delay at 2 and 4 years. *JAMA Pediatrics, 177*(10). htt ps://doi.org/10.1001/jamapediatrics.2023.3057

Tan, L., & Martin, G. (2014). Taming the adolescent mind: A randomised controlled trial examining clinical efficacy of an adolescent mindfulness-based group programme. *Child and Adolescent Mental Health, 20*(1), 49–55. https://doi.org/10.1111/camh.12057

Tantrums, tears, and tempers: Behavior is communication. (n.d.). Pacer Center. https://www.pacer.org/parent/php/php-c154.pdf

Teaching students with ADHD - Online resource kit: Differentiation for ADHD students. (n.d.). Online Resource Kit. http://onlineresourcekit-a dhd.blogspot.com/p/differentiating-curriculum-teaching.html

Teachkloud. (2023, December 3). *Understanding holistic development in early childhood: A comprehensive guide.* Teach Kloud. https://teachkloud.com/play-pedagogy-and-curriculum/understanding -holistic-development-in-early-childhood-a-comprehensive-guide/

Teglasi, H., Cohn, andrea, & Meshbesher, N. (2004). Temperament and learning disability. *Learning Disability Quarterly, 27*(1), 9–20. https://doi.org/10.2307/1593628

10 tips for supporting a child with ADHD. (2024, January 31). University Hospitals. https://www.uhhospitals.org/blog/articles/2024/01/10-tips-for-supporting-a-child-with-adhd

The children's behavior questionnaire. (n.d.). Bowdoin. https://research.bowdoin.edu/rothbart-temperament-questionnaires/instrument-descriptions/the-childrens-behavior-questionnaire/

The impact of ADHD on parent-child relationships and strategies for building strong bonds. (n.d.). HSMH. https://www.hsmh.co.uk/blog-posts/the-impact-of-adhd-on-parent-child-relationships-and-strategies-for-building-strong-bonds#:~:text=ADHD%20can%20undoubtedly%20impact%20parent

The infant behavior questionnaire (IBQ and IBQ-R). (n.d.). Bowdoin. https://research.bowdoin.edu/rothbart-temperament-questionnaires/instrument-descriptions/the-infant-behavior-questionnaire/

Thomas, A., & Chess, S. (1977). *Temperament and development.* Brunner/Mazel Publisher.

Thomas, N., & Karuppali, S. (2022). The efficacy of visual activity schedule intervention in reducing problem behaviors in children with Attention-Deficit/Hyperactivity Disorder between the age of 5 and 12 years: A systematic review. *Journal of the Korean Academy of Child and Adolescent Psychiatry, 33*(1), 2–15. https://doi.org/10.5765/jkacap.210021

Thompson, R. A., Winer, A. C., & Goodvin, R. (2013). *The individual child: Temperament, emotion, self, and personality.* 225–266. https://doi.org/10.4324/9780203813386-10

Tracy. (2015, June 20). *Temperament: Parent-child "fit."* Heart-Mind Online. https://heartmindonline.org/resources/temperament-parent-child-fit

Understanding children's behavior as communication. (2018, November 1). ECLKC. https://eclkc.ohs.acf.hhs.gov/mental-health/article/understanding-childrens-behavior-communication

Understanding temperament. (n.d.). ECCP https://www.eccpct.com/Resources/Child/Tips-for-Tots/Understand-Temperament-in-Young-Children/

Usher, C. (1989, November). The four humors or temperaments. *Lute Society of America Quarterly, 24*(4), 9–16. https://www.academia.edu/12353853/The_Four_Humors_or_Temperaments

van der Putten, A. A. J., Dijkstra, R. D., Huls, J. J., & Visser, L. (2017). Assessment of temperament in children with profound intellectual and multiple disabilities. A pilot study into the role of motor disabilities in instruments to measure temperament. *Cogent Psychology, 4*(1). https://doi.org/10.1080/23311908.2017.1335038

Varambally, S., Srinath, S., Gangadhar, B., Hariprasad, V., & Arasappa, R. (2013). Feasibility and efficacy of yoga as an add-on intervention in attention deficit-hyperactivity disorder: An exploratory study. *Indian Journal of Psychiatry, 55*(7), 379. https://doi.org/10.4103/0019-5545.116317

Weber, M. (2020, November). *Childhood insomnia and sleep problems.* Help Guide. https://www.helpguide.org/articles/sleep/childhood-insomnia-and-sleep-problems.htm

What you can learn from observing children. (2022, February 17). IACET. https://www.iacet.org/news/iacet-blog/blog-articles/what-you-can-learn-from-observing-children/

White, J. D. (1999). Review personality, temperament and ADHD. *Personality and individual differences, 27*(4), 589–598. https://doi.org/10.1016/s0191-8869(98)00273-6

Willis, A. (2024, February 5). *Classroom comfort: The role of environmental factors in supporting ADHD students.* Mississippi Association of Educators. https://www.maetoday.org/new-from-mae/classroom-comfort-role-environmental-factors-supporting-adhd-students

World Health Organization: WHO. (2019, April 24). *To grow up healthy, children need to sit less and play more.* World Health Organization. https://www.who.int/news-room/detail/24-04-2019-to-grow-up-healthy-children-need-to-sit-less-and-play-more

Zeigler, C. (2008, July 24). *How teachers can help every student shine.* ADDitude. https://www.additudemag.com/teaching-strategies-for-students-with-adhd/

Zentner, M., & Shiner, R. L. (2012). *Handbook of temperament.* Guilford Press. https://books.google.co.in/books?hl=en&lr=&id=bxHlV2UeXwYC&oi=fnd&pg=PA209&dq=assessing+temperament+in+children&ots=tWroDNrDhm&sig=uoy2KVrg7MJHL1Vi_65uZkM4C2k#v=onepage&q=assessing%20temperament%20in%20children&f=false

Zisopoulou, T., & Varvogli, L. (2022). Stress management methods in children and adolescents – Past, present, and future. *Hormone Research in Paediatrics, 96*(1). https://doi.org/10.1159/000526946

Made in the USA
Monee, IL
02 October 2024

67093952R00085